Through the Doors of the

Mission Inn

VOLUME TWO

BY

J O A N H . H A L L

HIGHGROVE PRESS
P.O. BOX 52888
RIVERSIDE, CA 92517-0888

ISBN 0-9631618-3-0

Library of Congress Catalog Card Number 00-134636

Printed in the United States of America – Riverside, California

To David with
best wishes

Joan H. Hall

Frank Miller and his pet macaws Joseph and Napoleon.

CONTENTS

PREFACE

Volume Two is a continuing account of a variety of distinctive people who have passed through the doors of the Mission Inn since 1876. This diverse group includes prominent statesmen, authors, actors, artists and conventional travelers, each with individual reasons for visiting Riverside.

The following narratives of randomly selected subjects provide brief life sketches and relates their Mission Inn experiences. This is not a collection of biographies, however, but rather a loose framework of time and circumstances reflecting little known past events.

Some entertaining characters include Congressman William McKinley, women activists Susan B. Anthony, Helen Keller and Carrie Nation. Another prominent guest was Albert Einstein whose impromptu visit abruptly terminated when he was injured by an aggressive macaw named Joseph. During the 1930s, movie stars Mary Pickford, Buddy Rogers and Cary Grant were hotel guests and many years later they individually revisited the hotel to recall happy memories. Will Rogers, Jack Lemmon, Judy Garland and Jack Benny also visited the Inn, each with different purposes.

1

My sources of information include items from newspaper files, public documents, literary histories and recollections of two former hotel employees. The Riverside Local History Resource Center, RLHRC, provided additional photographs and documented material. Surprisingly, unrelated facts, subjects and events often divulged new chapters to Riverside's history.

Frank Miller created the Mission Inn with its hospitable surroundings and a divergent group of guests were attracted to his hotel. As manager of the Loring Opera House he became acquainted with famous entertainers and renowned lecturers. His friendships and generosity extended to people from all walks of life and some of those not so famous characters are included in the following accounts.

Regardless of changing times, and some turbulent years, the Mission Inn has survived and continues to be one of Riverside's greatest assets under the supervision of its present owner Duane R. Roberts.

To the many guests, as well as visitors and residents of Riverside, I hope that you find the following individuals entertaining and enjoy a passing glimpse at some of the famous and not so famous people who have passed through the doors of the Mission Inn.

J.H.

Chapter 1

WILLIAM MC KINLEY
1843-1901

On a bright spring day in May 1881, a distinguished gentleman and two dignified ladies arrived in Riverside by stage. They registered at the Glenwood Hotel as Congressman William McKinley from Canton, Ohio, his wife Ida and his sister Anna McKinley. The McKinleys looked forward to their stay at the four-year-old Glenwood after reading numerous articles claiming "it is the loveliest place in southern California." The congressman hoped that the warmer climate and wholesome atmosphere might revitalize his frail, sickly wife. Accounts had described the hotel as a two-story house with a wide vine-covered porch, arranged so that guests could enjoy fresh air daily, ideal for the sick and weary. Several well-ventilated rooms on the ground floor accommodated invalids. The grounds covered an entire city block and the property was landscaped with fruit trees and shrubbery. Linen tablecloths and fine silverware were used in the dining room where healthy home cooked meals were served. Rates were $2 per day or $7 per week for room and board.

During the McKinleys visit, Glenwood owner Frank Miller and his wife Isabella were in Wisconsin visiting relatives and management of the hotel was left in the capable hands of his sister, Alice Miller. She proved to be a gracious hostess, introducing them to other distinguished guests including Henry E. Huntington, nephew of the railroad tycoon, Collis Huntington. Although a railroad line had not yet reached Riverside, an increasing number of travelers found their way to the Glenwood by other means. After several days of complete rest, the McKinleys returned to San Francisco and made connections to their home in Canton.

McKinley had lived in Canton since 1867, the same year he passed the state bar examination. A native of Niles, Ohio, he enlisted in the Union army during the Civil War and rose to the rank of major, a title he carried with pride for the remainder of his life. Following the war his spinster sister Anna, 12 years his senior and a public school principal, encouraged him to continue his education and provided the finances to earn his law degree. At her urging he established his law practice in Canton and they maintained a close relationship throughout the years.

As a young lawyer, he became a joiner, a moving force in the community. A deeply religious man, he was known for his honesty and personal charm. He belonged to the Methodist Church and had a persuasive talent as a public speaker and supported the popular temperance movement endorsed by the Women's Christian Temperance Union even though females could not vote.

After several years in Canton, William McKinley fell in love with a charming young lady named Ida Saxton. The attractive daughter of a local banker, she attended a prestigious finishing school in Pennsylvania and worked briefly in her father's bank. In 1871, Ida Saxton and William McKinley were married and their sedate church wedding was Canton's grandest social event of the year. The happy couple eventually had two daughters, their only children, both of whom died in early childhood. These tragedies caused Ida McKinley to develop a nervous condition that intensified her headaches and epileptic seizures. She settled into a sedentary invalid state, content to have her devoted husband take care of her.

At the age of 34, William McKinley was elected to Congress on the Republican ticket. Politics became his avocation and he slowly cultivated the distinctive talent of relating to the average, middle class American. When the McKinleys moved to Washington, they settled into a suitable hotel where, when necessary, Ida could entertain with little effort. It was common practice for elected politicians to live in residential hotels and this was especially convenient for Ida McKinley and her busy husband. They seldom accepted social invitations due to Ida's many illnesses, which were common knowledge and never concealed from the public. Whenever they did attend a social affair, however, seating arrangements had to be made in advance for Ida to be seated next to her husband in the event that she experienced an unexpected seizure. If this did occur, he carefully placed his napkin over her face until the seizure was over. William McKinley, in his matter-of-fact fashion, refused to talk about his wife's dispositions and affectionately took care of her in his own gentlemanly manner. Nevertheless, there were times when Ida rallied to the occasion and attended important events appearing to be a helpless Victorian female. Rather than stand in a receiving line for long periods of time, she would occasionally greet guests from a chair with a bouquet in her hands eliminating the need to shake hands with strangers.

William McKinley was considered an honest, hard working congressman. In 1890 he returned to Ohio and became governor. After serving two terms he emerged as a national figure and a candidate for president of the United States. On May 18, 1896, the chairman of the California Republican State convention announced the selection of Frank Miller as a member of the executive committee "in whose hands rest the management of the coming presidential campaign." Within weeks, Miller went to San Francisco and joined the California delegation that traveled to St. Louis for the Republican convention. On June 18 bells rang throughout Riverside signifying news that William McKinley had been nominated for President of the United States on the Republican ticket.

Several political clubs organized in Riverside to support and rally around William McKinley. Frank Miller had two huge flags made displaying McKinley's name and placed one on top of the Loring Opera House he managed and one on the Glenwood Hotel that he owned. In June 1896, local parades, speeches and benefits were held to endorse McKinley. A McKinley Club was organized and later another group established a First Time Voters party to insure a McKinley vote. The Riverside Afro-American Republican Club also organized with members meeting twice a month to get out the vote. While Republicans across the nation were working to put their candidate in office, William McKinley refused to leave his wife for long periods and instead conducted a "front porch" campaign and stayed close to home.

Even though he remained in Ohio, he gained the attention of distant supporters who were prospecting for gold in Alaska. These prospectors craved for any news from home. They lived and worked in the coldest temperatures on earth in areas permanently covered in snow. To honor William McKinley, these adventuresome men named a tall, snow-capped mountain Mount Mc Kinley. As the tallest peak in North America, called the top of the Continent, it rises more than 20,000 feet and is visible for hundreds of miles. A small trading station in the vicinity was later named Fairbanks to honor Charles Fairbanks, a good friend and confidant of McKinley.

As election day approached, Frank Miller installed a special telegraph wire to the Loring Opera House in order to receive election returns as soon as possible. On the stage were tables for committee workers and newspapermen and a large bulletin board to display incoming election returns. Arrangements were made for a local band to play between announced returns and the public was invited to attend for a nominal fee. Admission to the gallery was 10 cents and the best seats in the house went for a quarter.

Because of the huge local interest in the election, a big crowd filled the Loring. Every time a favorable return was posted on the bulletin board, loud applause followed and the band played a fast, patriotic tune. On November 5, the day after the election, local newspapers printed, "William McKinley was given a majority of 500 votes over William J. Bryan in Riverside County for the Presidency of the United States." The local McKinley Marching Band sent a box of Riverside navel oranges to congratulate the new President and the gift was later acknowledged by a letter of appreciation from his secretary.

During the McKinley administration the United States became a world power gaining control over the Hawaiian Islands, Puerto Rico, Guam and the Philippine Islands. After the Spanish-American War in 1898, two notable war heroes emerged, George Dewey and Theodore Roosevelt. When President McKinley ran for his second term in 1900, Roosevelt was his vice-presidential running mate. The Republicans won the election, but the President did not complete his term of office.

On September 6, 1901, while McKinley was addressing a crowd in Buffalo, New York, an anarchist named Leon Czolgosz shot him in the stomach. The best doctors and surgeons in the country tried to save the President but he died seven days later. During this trying ordeal, Ida McKinley proved stronger than anyone thought possible as she stayed by her husband's side to comfort him.

When news of McKinley's death reached Riverside, slowly ringing church bells were heard throughout the town. American flags on the Loring Opera House and on the Glenwood Hotel flew at half-staff in memory of a dignified gentleman who once visited Riverside as a little known Congressman and who ultimately became the 25th President of the United States. Towns across the nation later erected statues in tribute to the late president and parks and schools were named in his honor.

The McKinley home in Canton, Ohio, has been restored recently and is known as the Ida Saxton McKinley House. The three-story Victorian style structure, christened the First Ladies Library, holds memorabilia, photographs and bibliographies of the women who served in the

White House. In addition to first ladies these subjects include other White House hostesses such as Theodore Roosevelt's daughter Helen who took over the duties when her mother suffered a stroke and Grover Cleveland's sister who acted as White House hostess until her bachelor brother married Frances Folsom.

At one time the McKinley home was condemned but a grand-nephew of Ida McKinley saved it from the wrecking ball. The Stark Community Foundation, a philanthropic endowment organization, raised funds for restoration and the living first ladies became honorary chairpersons. Today the authentically restored house is the only educational institution focused on the life and times of America's first ladies and White House hostesses.

Four months after Congressman McKinley visited the Glenwood Hotel, Collis Huntington signed the register. His trip was strictly business.

Chapter 2

COLLIS POTTER HUNTINGTON
1821-1900

When the great railroad tycoon Collis Huntington registered at the Glenwood Hotel on September 18, 1881, he wrote CPRR (Central Pacific Rail Road) next to his name to identify himself. Alice Miller, the hotel manager and flawless hostess made certain everything met with his satisfaction. The 60-year-old Huntington exercised tremendous power throughout the nation both financially and politically. His brief, unannounced visit to the Glenwood was to observe the progress of the Santa Fe line then under construction from San Diego to San Bernardino. The Santa Fe Railroad was Huntington's major competitor and he utilized numerous legal and physical obstacles to interfere and delay any of their projects.

The Santa Fe route from San Diego passed inland through Box Springs Grade east of downtown Riverside. Unexpected road changes and expensive delays had plagued the Santa Fe construction and Collis Huntington wanted to view the situation first hand. An astute businessman and opportunist, he had been an independent entrepreneur since childhood.

Huntington had received little formal education in his early years in Connecticut. However, at age 14, he was supporting himself by selling watches and clocks. Later, he and his brother Solon opened a general store in New York. After gold was discovered in California, they began shipping goods to the gold fields. Collis Huntington soon developed gold fever, headed west and ultimately experienced great hardships crossing the Isthmus of Panama. After arriving in California, he settled in Sacramento near the gold fields and opened a hardware store in a tent where he sold mining supplies. The mercantile business proved very profitable and he soon took in a partner named Mark Hopkins. Hopkins turned out to be a frugal bookkeeper and a shrewd businessman. Together these two hard working men operated a prosperous hardware business for ten years and amassed a fortune.

In 1861, Collis Huntington joined three other Sacramento businessmen and incorporated the Central Pacific Railroad Company of

California. Leland Stanford with his law degree became president of the company; Huntington became vice-president, Mark Hopkins treasurer and Charles Crocker supervised construction. These diverse men became known as the Big Four. Regardless of their different backgrounds, the four worked as a unit and successfully operated the gigantic railroad project under difficult circumstances.

Although the nation was engulfed in Civil War, the government passed the Pacific Railroad Act in July 1862 providing for construction of a railroad and telegraph line from the Missouri River to the Pacific Ocean. The Central Pacific Railroad was awarded the contract to construct the road from the West Coast eastward to connect with the tracks of the Union Pacific. The government awarded large land grants and financed bonds for construction of the transcontinental railroad in order to open the west for settlement.

When the Central Pacific and Union Pacific tracks joined at Promontory, Utah, on May 11, 1869, the difficult journey west became history. After completion of the transcontinental connection, Collis Huntington and his three associates took over the Southern Pacific Railroad and established headquarters in San Francisco. Elaborate travel brochures and captivating stories were circulated in the eastern states to stimulate western passenger business and to entice new residents to settle on railroad land. Charles Nordhoff, a talented eastern newspaperman, wrote a popular book about the easy journey to California on the transcontinental train and reported on all the wonderful sights to be seen along the picturesque route. Huntington hired journalists to promote the numerous benefits of settling in California with the shrewd expectation of making huge profits from selling railroad land obtained by government grants. Furthermore, the farmland would hopefully produce products that required shipping and freight rates could be extremely profitable. Nordhoff and other writers described the best crops to grow in specific locations and provided detailed soil, water and climate information. Great animosity developed across the country about the controlling influence of big railroad companies especially the all-powerful owners of the Central Pacific and its successor the Southern Pacific Railroad. Failure to pay taxes, ill treatment of laborers and bloated freight rates added to the resentment directed toward the Big Four. In 1885, Collis Huntington ousted Leland Stanford as president of the Southern Pacific claiming he spent too little time with railroad business after becoming a United States Senator. He appointed himself president and his nephew Henry, Solon's son, as vice-president.

Huntington spent most of his time in New York where he lived comfortably with his wife Elizabeth Stoddard. A year after her death in 1883, he married Arabella, rumored to be his mistress, and adopted her young son, Archer. The Collis Huntingtons enjoyed a lavish lifestyle and maintained a number of residences. One was a grand mansion on San Francisco's Nob Hill near the ornate homes of Leland Stanford, Mark Hopkins and Charles Crocker. Whenever any of the Big Four wished to travel, there were a number of private deluxe Pullman cars available and their entourage had the right-of-way over scheduled passenger trains and lengthy freight cars. Pullman Palace cars were decorated lavishly with beautiful woodwork, handmade carpets, colorful draperies and separate compartments. Skilled chefs prepared elaborate meals served on fine china by accommodating waiters. These spectacular private cars became symbols of wealth and status and the affluent Huntingtons traveled in the most pretentious cars available. Arabella and Collis Huntington crossed the United States frequently but often traveled to Europe where Mrs. Huntington mingled with the international social set. She preferred Paris and New York to California.

When Huntington visited Riverside again in March 1897, he brought his wife Arabella, his nephew Henry and a party of officials from the Southern Pacific. They traveled in four separate Palace cars named *Director's Car, Otsego, Onesonta and Onesonta II.* Waiting carriages took the visitors on an extensive sightseeing tour of the area. They traveled down Magnolia Avenue and inspected the adjacent citrus groves and enjoyed the fragrance of blossoming navel orange trees. The carriages went around the outskirts of town and many inquisitive local residents wondered if they were investigating future railroad sites. The select party drove through downtown Riverside and stopped briefly to admire the grounds of the Glenwood Hotel. Collis Huntington's guests leisurely returned to their Pullman cars and traveled back to Los Angeles. The scheming head of the Southern Pacific decided Riverside might have a lucrative future. He then considered expanding his railroad to the community and set about plotting how best to expedite this neglected market.

The following year the Southern Pacific Railroad applied for a

Riverside franchise to operate standard gauge train tracks on the east side of Market Street to a proposed depot between Seventh and Eighth streets. The franchise was first adopted, then rescinded and city trustees listened for weeks to lively discussions, first favoring then opposing the ordinance. Frank Miller believed it unwise to fight the Southern Pacific, or any other railroad, in the interest of the community. He claimed the railroads helped the city's two most important businesses, the citrus industry and tourism.

The Southern Pacific wanted to extend its tracks to Eleventh Street where a turn- table could reverse cars back to the station and onward to eastern tracks. But a large contingent of citizens opposed the extension complaining the tracks and switches would be a menace, a blight on the beauty of the city. A petition of some 600 signatures asked the Riverside Board of Trustees to rescind the franchise to the Southern Pacific. There were denials of any discrimination against the railroad and lively discussions became lengthy and emotional. An out going Board of Trustees passed the required ordinance and the same day, the new Board of Trustees revoked it. There was much speculation as to the legality of the vote. Nevertheless, on Thursday May 27, at midnight, a Southern Pacific crew quietly went to work and extended their tracks to Eleventh Street. Many downtown residents condemned the high handed actions of the railroad and were incensed with Collis Huntington and the power he exerted.

City trustees finally granted the Southern Pacific franchise but work on the proposed depot was delayed for months. Collis Huntington sent his nephew Henry to Riverside on January 8, 1898, to look into the matter and ten days later a sizeable crew of men began excavating the depot's foundation. Teams of mules hauled the unwanted dirt to nearby construction trains and lumber was piled up on the site ready for use. While the depot was still under construction, Huntington wasted no time in advertising and started an aggressive campaign to inform the public of the several new transcontinental routes.

Flamboyant ads appeared daily in local newspapers publicizing inexpensive excursions to San Francisco and the daily Pullman Buffet Sleeper through to Chicago in four days and four nights. This run was scheduled to arrive in Chicago in time to make all eastern connections eliminating the expense of an overnight hotel. In addition, the company extended their service on the *Sunset Limited* to New Orleans with a vestibule sleeper and a dining car with meals a la carte. Every Friday a train left Riverside for Pittsburgh via New Orleans, Memphis and Cincinnati and advertised low rates and modern sleeping car accommodations. Travelers were advised to contact the Southern Pacific ticket office at the Glenwood on Main Street. The company printed attractive brochures explaining "the easy way to see California" with half tone illustrations of points of interest. Riverside was well portrayed in their advertising with beautiful photos of Magnolia Avenue and acres of citrus trees.

Through the spring and summer of 1898, crews of men worked on the new depot and train tracks along Market Street. When completed, the Southern Pacific depot was the first Mission Revival style building in Riverside. A sweeping tile roof extended 16 feet over walls of decorative pressed brick and created a covered, arched walkway around the building. Graveled walks were interspersed with flowerbeds that added to the attractiveness and accessibility to the building. Inside, a large waiting room covered most of the main floor with baggage space in the back of the lobby. A huge portrait of Collis Huntington was displayed in the railroad agent's office. The Southern Pacific Company had spent over $10,000 on the beautiful building and the public derived many benefits from its location in Riverside.

During Collis Huntington's long rule over various railroad companies, he built many stations and warehouses that were little more than shacks. This controversial character, however, introduced a new style of architecture to Riverside when he built the Southern Pacific station. The classic building served the city for many years, first as a train station and later as a centrally located Pacific Electric streetcar terminal.

Collis Huntington provided the means for people to travel west and an eastern journalist named Charles Nordhoff mythologized California. Both men made it possible for the famous and not so famous people to pass through the doors of the Mission Inn.

Chapter 3

CHARLES NORDHOFF
1830-1901

On September 23, 1881, five days after the departure of Collis Huntington, Charles Nordhoff, a New York newspaperman, signed the Glenwood Hotel register. It was his second visit to Riverside and he was amazed at the growth of the town in the nine years since his earlier visit. At that time, the Miller family had not yet moved to California and the Glenwood Hotel did not exist. On both occasions Nordhoff was in search of regional information for his travel books on western points of interest.

Nordhoff's first travel book, published in 1872 by Harper & Brothers was entitled *California for Health, Pleasure and Residence* and filled 250 pages with descriptions of what to expect while traveling west aboard a luxurious Pullman car. He reported the fare from New York to San Francisco as $500 plus a dollar per meal. The trip took seven days on "the big iron horse" that averaged 39 miles per hour. He listed names of some good San Francisco hotels with accommodations ranging from $2 to $3.50 a day. The most convenient method of reaching southern California was aboard an overnight steamer, costing $18, that docked in San Pedro. Nordhoff took this route south and proceeded inland to the San Bernardino Valley.

He found the region an excellent place for farming with good soil and ample water. His commentary included a brief visit to the nearby community of Riverside, a two-year-old planned colony, but he did not recommend settlement on the treeless plain. With less than 50 families living on the edge of a desert, Nordhoff believed the place was doomed to fail and the town would not survive. Although he held out little hope for the colony, he implied the dry air and even temperature might benefit those suffering from consumption.

His first travel book became a best seller due to its timely publication and to the author's careful attention to details. Before completion of the transcontinental railroad in 1869, options for traveling west were limited to overland journeys by wagon or by steamboat via the Isthmus of Panama. These long trips entailed great hardships plagued by danger, disease and discomfort. Railroads offered a fast, safe, comfortable means of traveling west and the New York journalist found the experience exciting and exhilarating. Charles Nordhoff thrived on adventure and his entire life had been one interesting experience after another.

Nordhoff was born in Prussia where his father served in the German army until he was exiled for his liberalism. In 1834, the family moved to America and settled in the Mississippi Valley where they lived comfortably in the remote wilderness. When Charles and Adelheid Nordhoff died suddenly leaving young Charles an orphan, Bishop Nast of Cincinnati became his guardian. At age 13, he was apprenticed to a printer for a year and worked on a Philadelphia newspaper. He joined the navy in 1844 and during his three years there he sailed around the world and discovered the sea stimulating and invigorating. After leaving the navy, he spent several years sailing on fishing and whaling ships based in New England. His adventuresome life as a sailor provided an abundance of remarkable background material that he later incorporated in 13 best selling books.

Charles Nordhoff worked from 1853 to 1871 as a writer and editor for the *New York Evening Post* and the *New York Herald*. He married and his only son Walter was born in 1855. While working for the newspapers he found time to publish a three volume series of books recalling his exciting adventures at sea. These books established Nordhoff as a professional writer with literary talent. During the turbulent years of the Civil War, he was a Washington correspondent and covered the Union cause. Because he expressed his views in precise strong language he gained a vast following of readers. In 1871, at the age of 60, he left the newspaper and for the next several years devoted his time to traveling, especially in California and Hawaii.

When the transcontinental railroad was completed, Nordhoff discovered a new experience that he wished to share with the American public. Travel handbooks became a novel means of promoting tourism and a lucrative method of railroad advertising. Major rail lines encouraged western travel in an effort to sell their government granted land and to increase population for future profits. The Southern Pacific Railroad, controlled by Collis Huntington, hired Charles Nordhoff to write complimentary stories about the "glorious life to be found in sunny California." Colorful brochures pictured peaceful homes nestled among fruit bearing orange trees with majestic snow-capped mountains in the background. There were others who wrote of the wonders to be found in

California in addition to Charles Nordhoff. Marcus D. Boruck, one of many subsidized writers, managed a weekly San Francisco publication that was fully financed by the Southern Pacific Railroad. His book *Spirit of the Times* became a best seller. California was promoted around the world in extravagant publications and spectacular photographs. The California Immigrant Union advertised for settlers and encouraged one and all to move to the land of opportunity. Western newspapers and pamphlets distributed by railroad agents all aimed to entice prospective buyers to settle in designated areas primarily owned by railroad companies.

In 1874, a new town near Ventura was named Nordhoff to honor the prominent author who promoted the state. He had written, "I believe southern California to be the finest part of the state and the best region in the whole United States for farmers." The new town had a Nordhoff post office, two hotels and a hot springs advertised to benefit invalids. The region did not attract many settlers however and in 1917 the community gave way to nearby Ojai. Nonetheless, the name Nordhoff is still in use today and identifies some schools, parks and streets.

The written word reached more people than the regional railroad lectures and inviting railroad pictures. Charles Nordhoff's first book was such a huge success, it had several printings and revisions. Ten years after his initial visit to California, he returned to update his obsolete handbook and to add new information about the fast developing state. When he revisited Riverside in 1881, he was amazed at the systematic development that had taken place. There were several schools, a variety of churches and any number of substantial houses occupied by industrious families. Magnolia Avenue with its double drive neatly lined with leafy shade trees had become a well- known tourist attraction. Townspeople advocated and supported the temperance movement then gaining strength across the nation. There were hundreds of acres of grapes that were dried and packed as fancy Riverside raisins. Citrus groves flourished throughout the area and the grafted navel orange trees produced the best seedless fruit in the state. Charles Nordhoff was impressed with Riverside's development and now considered it to be one of the most desirable places to live. A farmer could make a decent living and at the same time enjoy the magnificent scenery and excellent climate. When he checked out of the Glenwood Hotel, his notebook was full of records and notes for his second travel book.

Charles Nordhoff's early travel books about California lured more people west than any other event, including the dramatic gold rush. He wrote, "There are no dangers to travelers in California and no inconveniences that a child or a tender woman would not laugh at. When you spend a few weeks in the State, you will return to New York with the notion it is a frontier land and California a completely civilized place." In addition his books gave hope to those suffering from consumption when he stated, "The purity of the air in Los Angeles is remarkable. The air, when inhaled, gives to the individual a stimulus and vital force which only an atmosphere so pure can ever communicate. The sky is blue, the sun unclouded and everyday of the year one can go out-of-doors." Nordhoff claimed California was the least expensive place to live in the United States because one could raise food while enjoying the good climate.

Charles Nordhoff retired as a newspaper editor and started a new adventure. In 1855, when his only son Warren was born, he acquired a large tract of land in Baja California from the Mexican International Company. It encompassed some fifty thousand acres of pristine coastal land south of Ensenada. In 1887, he transferred the property to his son Warren, who was then married and a new father. The magnanimous gift included paid up property taxes for 25 years. Warren's new baby boy was named Charles Bernard, much to the delight of his grandfather. When Nordhoff retired in 1890, he and his wife moved to Coronado, California to be near his family living at the old ranch house in Baja. He lived out his years in his favorite state overlooking his beloved Pacific Ocean. After his death in 1901, his adventure books became popular once again to a new generation of readers.

Charles Bernard Nordhoff, grandson of the journalist, grew up on the remote ranch in Baja but nevertheless received a good education in private schools. In 1909, he graduated from Harvard and a few years later, when war first broke out in Europe, he went to France to drive an ambulance. Young Charles became a pilot during World War I and while in France, teamed up with another American soldier named John Norman Hall. The two men were assigned to work on a history of the Lafayette Flying Corps and they established a routine of writing biographical stories of Americans who served in the French squadrons. After the war, the two former pilots remained close friends and in 1920 they sailed for

Tahiti to write a travel book about the South Sea Islands. Instead, they wrote three novels about the most famous mutiny in British naval history, *Mutiny on the Bounty, Men Against the Sea*, and *Pitcairn's Island*. These two authors wrote several other books and became well known for their adventure stories. Charles Bernard Nordhoff eventually lived in Redlands and Santa Barbara, reflecting his grandfather's enthusiasm for southern California.

Facts, figures and advice written by newspaperman Charles Nordhoff changed the lives of hundreds of people who moved west based on his words. These settlers were the pioneers who built towns, started businesses and made history that was later recorded and preserved by Hubert Howe Bancroft. Although Bancroft's visit to the Glenwood Hotel made little news, Riverside is included in his extensive work.

Chapter 4

JANE LATHROP STANFORD
1828-1905

During the spring of 1882, Mrs. Leland Stanford vacationed in southern California with her sister-in-law Mrs. Henry Lathrop, her 13-year-old son Leland Jr. and his tutor Harold Nash. They traveled in their luxurious Pullman car called *The Stanford* and stopped in Riverside to spend the night at the Glenwood Hotel. Jane Lathrop Stanford believed traveling an important supplement to her son's education and this was his first visit to Riverside. Young Leland, already a seasoned traveler, had lived in Europe for two years and frequently crossed the United States in one of his father's Central Pacific trains. Even though this was a casual overnight stay at the Glenwood, the Miller family made certain everything met with Mrs. Stanford's satisfaction. After all, this elite party chose to stay at the Miller's hotel rather than in their luxurious parlor car with all the comforts of home.

An addition to the Glenwood was taking place at the time but the hotel remained open for business and construction did not disturb guests. The new wing included 30 guestrooms, each with a private bath and an electric bell to summon assistance. Jane Stanford found the Glenwood accommodations quite adequate, clean and comfortable with wholesome, home cooked meals served by gloved waiters. The hotel's grandeur, however, was far below the standards and opulence of the Stanford's San Francisco mansion on Nob Hill, yet the Glenwood was much more pleasant and far superior to her first home in California.

Jane and Leland Stanford were married in Albany, New York in 1850 the year he passed the state bar. They both came from large families, Jane was one of seven children and Leland one of seven boys. Jane was devoted to her Lathrop family and had been reared as a refined young lady, frugal and accomplished in household management. She grew up admiring Queen Victoria, who was only nine years older, and often mimicked her appearance. All members in the Stanford family had received some form of education. When Leland began practicing, his father presented him a complete set of valuable law books, a gift he treasured. Unfortunately, a tragic fire destroyed his office building and he was unable to make a decent living without his law library. Leland's father encouraged him to go to California where two of his brothers, Josiah and Philip, had opened a general store in Sacramento near the gold fields. Pressure from both families kept Jane home with her parents due to stories of the hard life in the wild west, considered unsuitable for a refined Victorian lady. In 1852, Leland joined his brothers in California and worked there for three years while his wife Jane remained in Albany to nurse her sick father. Although they were thousands of miles apart, the dedicated couple wrote frequent letters that often took months to be delivered.

Leland Stanford returned to New York in 1855 after his father-in-law's death. The couple decided to move to California and settled in Sacramento. Housing was scarce and they stayed in a hotel until they found a simple two-room house to rent. Jane made do with little money and improvised furnishing for their first home by covering boxes for chairs and made wardrobes from curtains. Although their belongings were meager they both worked hard and saved money. When Leland Stanford's brothers moved to San Francisco, he bought their interest in the general store. Selling provisions, groceries, wine, liquor, cigars and all types of miner's supplies proved lucrative for the frugal couple who paid off family loans and accumulated a good nest egg.

In 1856, Leland Stanford became involved in politics and helped found the Republican Party in California. He ran for two state offices and was defeated each time. Jane Stanford did not object to his political career and he asked her advice and kept her informed about official matters. When he was elected governor in 1861, they moved into a four-year-old house in downtown Sacramento. The house was not a mansion when they first occupied it, however, and the Stanfords spent hundreds of dollars and made it into a show place. Later, in 1899, Jane Stanford donated the property to the Catholic Church.

In the meantime, Governor Leland Stanford became interested in the transcontinental railroad and joined Collis Huntington, Mark Hopkins and Charles Crocker in establishing the Central Pacific Railroad. As president of the company, Stanford turned the first dirt to begin the historic project in February 1863 and upon its completion in May 1869 drove in the last spike uniting the tracks. During these demanding years, he traveled frequently while Jane remained at home content to entertain her many lady friends and numerous visiting relatives. Between the Lathrop and Stanford families there were dozens of in-laws, nieces and nephews.

After 19 years of marriage, there was great rejoicing in 1868 when Leland Stanford Junior entered the world. Shortly after the birth of their baby, the Stanfords entertained close friends at a dinner party in their Sacramento home. During dinner, a large silver domed platter was placed in the center of the table and Leland Stanford rose from his chair, and with great pride said, "My friends, I wish to introduce my son to you." He ceremoniously lifted the lid to reveal tiny Leland carefully arranged on the silver platter. Each guest was introduced to the baby as the platter was passed around the table. The Stanfords were elated with their son and their devotion to their only child became legendary.

When baby Leland was a year old, he traveled across the United States with his parents aboard the new transcontinental railroad. This successful project made millions of dollars for all four men involved in its completion. Leland Stanford became president of the new Southern Pacific Railroad, successor to the Central Pacific, headquartered in San Francisco. In 1874 Stanford moved his family from Sacramento to San Francisco and had plans drawn for construction of an imposing mansion to be built on top of Nob Hill. The 40-room house located on the corner of Powell and California streets had a magnificent view and privacy. Construction of their San Francisco home took several years and during this time the family lived in the finest suite of America's first luxury hotel, the Palace.

The Stanfords went east to purchase furnishings and elegant decorations for their new home. They bought furniture to fill sitting rooms, billiard and library rooms and works of art for the entire house. Jane Stanford had her desk placed on the top floor where she could look out large windows to the City below. Occasionally the steep grade on Nob Hill gave her trouble when her horse couldn't pull her carriage to the top. Her devoted husband solved the problem by installing a cable car on the hill for her convenience. Young Leland and his mother were often the only passengers in the little car pulled up the hill by underground cables. The California Street Cable Railroad Company was incorporated in 1878 with the stipulation it could not interfere with ordinary wagon or carriage traffic.

To escape the summer fog in San Francisco, the Stanford's purchased property in Palo Alto and referred to it as the *Farm*. Here they enjoyed a more casual life in the country atmosphere and as a hobby they raised prize horses. *The Farm* was young Leland's favorite place, a home with outdoor activities and warm summer weather. His parents, however, were often sick and traveled to Europe frequently in search of miraculous cures for their many ailments. Whenever they went aboard, they stayed at exclusive resorts and spas, "taking the waters" in an effort to improve their poor health. In 1885, 15-year-old Leland came down with a fever while with his family in Florence. The best European doctors were summoned to his bedside in the Hotel Bristol and Catholic nuns nursed him around the clock. Cobbled streets nearby were covered with straw to deaden the noise made by metal wagon wheels so as not to disturb Leland. In spite of the best available medical attention, Leland Stanford Jr. died on March 14, 1884 of typhoid fever. Needless to say, his parents were devastated to lose their beloved only child.

His body was sent to New York where it remained while an appropriate mausoleum could be constructed at the *Farm*. As a memorial to their son, Jane and Leland Stanford decided to use their fortune for the benefit of young people and issued a joint statement; "Since the idea of establishing an institution for the benefit of mankind came directly and largely from our son, the institution shall bear his name and shall be known as the Leland Stanford Junior University." They donated seven thousand acres of land in Palo Alto as a site for the new college. On Leland Stanford Jr's 19th birthday, the cornerstone of the building was placed and the school officially opened October 1, 1887. David Starr Jordan, one of the leading scientists in the country, was selected by the Stanfords to be the first president of the university.

Leland Stanford was reelected a United States Senator in 1885 and Harold Nash, Leland Junior's former tutor, became the Senator's private secretary. While serving in the senate, the Stanfords acquired a suitable residence in Washington, D.C. where they entertained government dignitaries. They spent part of the year in the east, some time in San Francisco and in Palo Alto and continued to travel aboard. The strain of overwork and periods of depression affected the Senator's health and in 1893 he died. His burial took place on university grounds and good friends David Starr Jordan and Harold Nash comforted Jane Stanford in her grief.

Mrs. Stanford continued to travel and in 1895 she visited Riverside accompanied by her niece. The Southern Pacific's agent in Riverside escorted the ladies around town and Mrs. Stanford was impressed with the blooming, fragrant citrus groves. She said nothing in Europe could compare with Riverside's beautiful Magnolia Avenue including the famous drives in London and Paris.

In 1897, Jane Stanford attended Queen Victoria's 60th Jubilee in London. This was a lifetime thrill for her to see the Queen in all her splendor. She rented a complete floor of a building along the parade route in order to see the Queen on her way to St. Paul's Cathedral. From this vantage point she could observe the Queen's open carriage, the last one in the long procession. As the parade came to a halt in front of the cathedral, the Queen looked around at the crowd and then stared right at Mrs. Stanford. Victoria regally bowed her head toward her and Mrs. Stanford enthusiastically bowed in return, throwing a kiss to the Queen. It was a memorable experience Jane Stanford treasured the rest of he life.

The prolific writer and historian Hubert H. Bancroft wrote a scholarly book about the life of Leland Stanford and concluded few people really knew Jane Stanford. He believed her the source of her husband's power and claimed her common sense and strong character facilitated his numerous contributions bestowed to the state of California.

Ohio Congressman William McKinley passed through the doors of the Glenwood Hotel in 1881.

Collis Huntington the dynamic railroad tycoon appointed himself president of the Southern Pacific Railroad in 1885.

In 1898 Huntington's Southern Pacific Company erected a Mission style depot on Market between Seventh and Eighth streets.

J.H. Hall Collection

All aboard!

J.H. HALL COLLECTION

Fred Harvey enterprises still in business.

H.H. Bancroft collected historic material of the western United States.

Joseph Pulitzer favored construction of the proposed Rubidoux Hotel on Mount Rubidoux.

Riverside High School graduating class of 1892.

Thomas J. Murphy, Victor D. Noble, Edith G. Beamer, Prof. C.H. Keyes, (Superintendent of City Schools), Ray L. Wilbur, Fred Cuttle, Edith Easton, Ernest A. Meacham, Blanche Aberdein

Many famous people appeared on the stage of the Loring Opera House.

Eleven of Sanford Dole's thirteen Riverside nieces and nephews.

Susan B. Anthony appeared on the stage of the Loring Opera House in 1895.

Madame Helena Modjeska as she appeared in Mary Stuart.

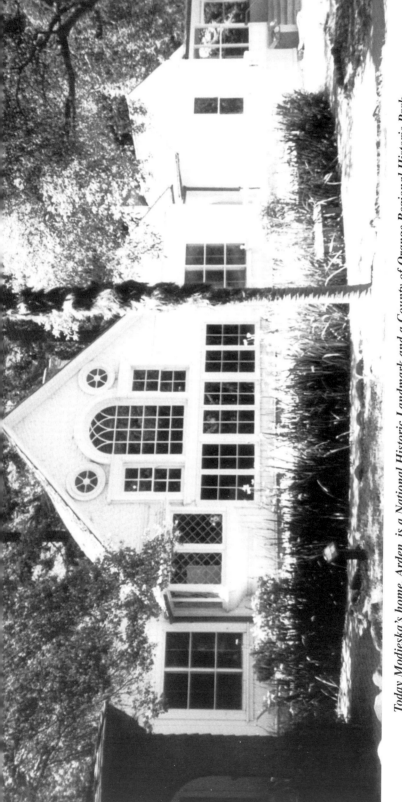

Today Modjeska's home, Arden, is a National Historic Landmark and a County of Orange Regional Historic Park.

Fanny Stevenson as she appeared in the South Pacific where she cared for her famous husband, Robert Louis Stevenson.

A grand reception to honor Mrs. Robert Louis Stevenson was held in the Jake Van de Grift home on Orange Street between Third and Fourth.

Frank Miller's pet birds received the best of care.

Chapter 5

FREDERICK HENRY HARVEY
1835-1901

In the fall of 1882, Fred Harvey and his wife joined friends from their hometown of Leavenworth, Kansas, for a sightseeing trip through southern California. The tourists arrived in Riverside on November 20 and registered at the Glenwood Hotel. Fred Harvey was a successful restaurateur who operated a chain of eating houses and hotels along the Atchison, Topeka and Santa Fe Railroad route. Even though this was considered to be a vacation for the industrious businessman, he couldn't resist inspecting restaurants and hotels included in their itinerary. Harvey was always searching for new techniques to incorporate into his thriving establishments.

The Glenwood Hotel, sometimes referred to as the Glenwood Cottage or Tavern, took on a new identity after Frank Miller's 1882 construction. The two-story wing, attached to the original family house, included a larger dining room and kitchen and separate servant quarters. The main entrance off Main Street opened into an eight-foot wide hallway that led to a newly furnished parlor and several adjacent reading rooms. On the second floor, there were 30 additional sleeping rooms, each with a private bathroom and electric bell to summon assistance. A broad veranda over both floors provided a sheltered walkway leading to public and private rooms. The attractive planted grounds surrounding the hotel included fruit trees and decorative arbors supporting climbing grapevines. Guests were encouraged to enjoy the garden fruit, especially during the winter months when navel oranges were in season. The Kansas tourists found the Glenwood a hospitable, comfortable hotel and an ideal place to relax before continuing to Los Angeles.

Fred Harvey and his traveling companions stayed at the finest hotel in Los Angeles, the Pico House, considered the grandest hotel in southern California with elegant reading and billiard rooms. Regardless of the Pico House reputation, Fred Harvey was greatly impressed with Riverside's Glenwood Hotel. The following year, his close friend and business partner, Captain Byron Schermerhorn spent the winter at the Glenwood Hotel on the recommendation of Fred Harvey.

Schermerhorn's doctor had informed him to seek a milder winter climate because he could not survive many more cold eastern seasons. Harvey was loyal and compassionate to his close friends and always remembered his own humble background.

Frederick Henry Harvey was born in England. At the age of 15 he came to the United States and supported himself by working as a kitchen dishwasher. He subsequently learned to manage a clean, efficient kitchen having worked all sorts of restaurant jobs. When he married his wife Barbara, they settled in Leavenworth, Kansas, and raised seven children. His work as a railroad agent required a great deal of traveling keeping him from his large family for long periods of time. In addition, Harvey took note of the poor quality of food and lack of comfort he experienced in his travels for the railroad. Most often passengers had to provide their own meals and it was common practice to cook outside wherever the train stopped. Inferior lunch stands and food vendors selling questionable food started to appear along the major railroad routes. Seasoned travelers soon learned not to buy this food. In 1872, Harvey decided to open his own restaurant in Topeka, Kansas, where he would serve quality home cooked food to appreciative passengers.

This venture was so successful that Harvey convinced the president of the Santa Fe line he could provide decent dining facilities and clean hotels to passengers all along their route. A binding and lasting agreement was struck in 1876 and the Fred Harvey Company was launched. The Harvey family worked together gathering furniture, good linens, china and silverware to equip the railroad restaurants. In a matter of seven years, the handsome little Englishman with a trimmed mustache and pointed goatee left his menial railroad job and successfully started the Harvey House chain of eating establishments. Business was so good he eventually hired diligent managers to operate his increasing number of restaurants.

Harvey House restaurants were located about 200 miles apart along the Santa Fe Railroad. The meals were comparable to most large eastern hotels and were served by attractive young ladies. These pretty waitresses, called Harvey Girls, wore demure uniforms and served traveling customers quickly and efficiently. They were recruited primarily from the Midwest through newspaper advertisements. The ads stipulated a potential employee had to be less than 30 years of age, of good character, attractive and intelligent. If hired, the ladies were taught to be courteous and patient and were required to live in chaperoned dormitories near their jobs. They earned $17.50 a month plus tips and board. Attired in uniforms of black dresses with white collars and aprons, their legs were covered in heavy black stockings and serviceable black shoes. Regardless of their plain, sedate outfits, Harvey Girls became wives to hundreds of western bachelors. Humorist Will Rogers once quipped, "Harvey kept the west in food and wives."

Harvey Girls had to provide quick service with a non-rushed attitude to keep the diners happy. As one Harvey girl took orders for drink preferences, another waitress followed immediately filling the order to the amazement of the customer. Special signals were relayed such as an inverted cup, or special placement of silverware to indicate an order of coffee with cream or sugar, iced tea or plain water. Passengers often ordered ahead of time and their menu choice would be telegraphed to the next Harvey House. Upon their arrival, their order was waiting for them. The quality of the food and the good, home style cooking also attracted local people who frequented the dining facilities. Harvey Houses had a rotating menu and customers looked forward to the variety of meals. Many single men ate all their meals at a Harvey House where they often befriended the attractive waitresses.

By the 1890s, the tourist trade increased tremendously and passengers began stopping at new Fred Harvey hotels for extended periods of time. The fear of losing valuable ticket sales stimulated the railroads to add dining cars to their long distance routes. The Fred Harvey Company provided service for 20 dining cars on the Santa Fe line. Even though travelers could comfortably eat aboard their trains, the Harvey restaurants and hotels continued to be profitable and kept increasing in numbers. Harvey provided comfortable lodgings and quality hospitality to a new western frontier once filled with historic Spanish missions and Indian villages. In response to this southwestern theme, his hotel and restaurant buildings began to reflect the architecture of earlier cultures. Indian motifs and objects were blended into the designs of these commercial buildings.

For years Native Americans tried to sell their handcrafted items to disembarking train passengers. Tourists were good customers who bought baskets, rugs and jewelry as souvenirs of their trips west. As railroads continued to bring more people to the southwest, Indian traders started selling poorly made artifacts to unsuspecting buyers. Many of these rugs and blankets were woven with cotton string in place of good sheep's wool and poor plant dyes were used for basket material. The expert craftsmanship of true artisans was replaced with inexpensive articles produced for the tourist trade. In response, the Fred Harvey Company opened gift shops and show rooms in many of their hotels and featured authentic Indian products for sale. The company encouraged artisans to produce quality items and tourists bought goods for a fair price to the satisfaction of all concerned. To induce sales and attract customers, the Harvey Company hired Indian craftsmen to demonstrate production of their products by setting up small workshops in their hotels. As potential buyers watched the artisans weaving a blanket or making a basket, they gained a greater appreciation of Indian artifacts.

Members of the Harvey family realized that many of the early Indian designs and art techniques were disappearing with each new generation. They began to collect rare, old pieces and retained much of the good traditional work they commissioned. Indian craftsmen were encouraged to copy the old colors and symbols displayed on ancient items in the Harvey collection. The Harvey family was one of the major forces responsible for revitalizing the good quality and authenticity of Indian workmanship. Their hotel gift shops were stocked with good Indian pieces and buyers came from all over the world to purchase genuine products. Fred Harvey's friend and partner, Byron Schermerhorn managed the main tourist route from Chicago to San Bernardino which Harvey officials considered the busiest and most lucrative line.

Captain Byron Schermerhorn managed 22 Harvey House restaurants along the Santa Fe route. His good friend Fred Harvey named one of his sons Byron, a name that has remained in the family for several generations. When Schermerhorn retired in the late 1880's, he was a wealthy man and he traveled through Europe for a number of years. Later, due to poor health, he began to spend his winters in southern California at the Glenwood Hotel. Captain Schermerhorn probably knew Frank Miller's father, C. C. Miller, also a captain in the Civil War. Schermerhorn liked the town of Riverside and bought several citrus groves as investments. In May 1892, he died suddenly in his room at the Glenwood and Millers informed his wife and two daughters living in the east. One of his daughters purchased a burial plot in Riverside's Evergreen Cemetery adjacent to the Miller family plot. Christopher Columbus Miller, Frank's father, had died two years before but no marker had been placed on his grave. When the Schermerhorn family commissioned an engraver to inscribe their family name on a large gray granite marker, they had added C. C. Miller's name. One side of the gravestone displayed the Grand Army of the Republic emblem and on the opposite side the symbol of the Knights of Templer. The old marker near the corner of Fourteenth and Cedar still stands in the historic cemetery.

Fred Harvey died in February 1901 at his home in Leavenworth, Kansas. His enterprises included 47 restaurants, 30 dining cars and 15 hotels. The 66-year-old gentleman had started a successful business that continued to grow bigger and more important even after his death. Family members took over his prosperous operations and expanded the Harvey chain of hotels and restaurants. Most of the famous, classic structures known today as Harvey Houses were actually constructed after Fred Harvey's death. Nonetheless, Elbert Hubbard, founder of the Roycroft Arts and Crafts colony in East Aurora, New York, eulogized Harvey as " a civilizer and benefactor whose name is a symbol of all that is beautiful and useful".

Chapter 6

HUBERT HOWE BANCROFT
1832-1918

During the great boom years of the 1880s, H. H. Bancroft traveled through the western states collecting information relating to the early development and history of that portion of the United States. His collection of western frontier ephemera was heralded as the finest in the nation and yet he continued to accumulate more documents, old maps and regional newspapers. In November 1887, Bancroft arrived in Riverside and registered at the Glenwood Hotel. His traveling partners were Edwin W. Fowler general manager of the Bancroft History Publishing Company and H. L. Wilson, his personal secretary. These three gentlemen were in town on business and spent the day interviewing prominent citizens and recording memories of some early settlers. They gathered as much information as possible to add to the extensive history library in San Francisco owned by Hubert H. Bancroft.

With real estate exchanging hands rapidly, and new towns and subdivisions created daily, Bancroft was attempting to chronicle the chain of events then making history. Although Los Angeles was in the center of the greatest growth, Riverside promoted its abundant water supply and famous raisin and citrus industries. These agricultural attributes had attracted new settlers to the community and Bancroft was anxious to note the recent changes taking place in Riverside. Five years earlier, canvassing agents representing the W. W. Elliott Company had come to town to get advanced subscriptions for a book to be published entitled *The History of San Bernardino County*. Elliott traveled to San Bernardino, Redlands, Riverside and Colton to gather information for his book and solicit advance orders to pay for its printing. To increase sales he included San Diego County and hired C. C. Cook to illustrate important buildings and prominent people. The 1883 book was the first published "mug" book about Riverside and it became another volume added to Bancroft's history library.

H. H. Bancroft was six feet tall, with dark hair combed across his forehead framing his serious dark eyes. His average appearance did not betray his scholarly demeanor and nothing about his personality revealed his creative ability. When he visited the Glenwood Hotel in 1887, his reputation had already been established as a prolific writer, eminent historian and owner of the finest western history library in the nation. Ironically, his passion for books began as a small business venture when he was still a teenager in Buffalo, New York.

As a young boy, he went to work for his brother-in-law, George H. Derby, who owned a bookstore and print shop in Buffalo. He was assigned to the lowly bindery department and his apparent dissatisfaction prompted his dismissal. His brother-in-law gave him money to return home to Ohio and incidentally supplied him with several cases of books to sell on consignment. Young Bancroft sold the books quickly and with the profits, paid off his debts and had money left over. In 1850 his father and brothers caught "gold fever" and set off for California to make their fortunes prospecting. Eighteen-year-old Bancroft returned to Buffalo to work in the print shop where he earned one hundred dollars a year. He learned the business of printing, binding and publishing books and acquired the skill of selling the finished product. Derby began to wonder if there might not be a substantial book market involving the miners in California. He convinced young Bancroft to personally analyze the book market in the west and to determine the best location to sell his merchandise. Derby sent $5,000 worth of books to San Francisco for Bancroft to peddle while investigating the potential book market.

In February 1852, the young 20-year-old set off for California by steamer to Panama where he traveled months to reach the Pacific Coast. Heavy freight, such as crates of books, were shipped around the tip of South America and up the coast to San Francisco. When Bancroft arrived in California, he visited his father and brothers who were mining near the Feather River. He helped them for eight months, until his brother-in-law's books arrived in San Francisco. Bancroft sent the crates of books to Sacramento where weary miners eagerly purchased the entire lot. Even though this transaction was a great success, H. H. Bancroft returned to Buffalo to help his sister when George Derby died. After a year or two in Buffalo, he returned to California to make his own fortune. Due to his first western book selling experiences, Bancroft was extended credit to open his own shop.

The firm of H. H. Bancroft & Company opened for business in San Francisco on December 1, 1856. Open cases of books were nicely displayed in front of his rented store on Montgomery Street. He routinely replaced the books with new stock thereby acquiring new customers and developing a special clientele. The proprietor slept on a cot behind the counter to save money and consequently remained open for business well into the night. Because of Bancroft's selection of good books, and his superior salesmanship, business prospered and he soon outgrew the small store. He moved into a three story building and hired several employees to assist in the growing book business. Bancroft's younger brother Albert came to work for the company and proved to be a great asset to Hubert Howe Bancroft.

By 1859, another store opened and this one specialized in stationery and paper products. It was managed by Albert Bancroft and later consolidated under the name A. L. Bancroft. Regardless of the firm's name, H. H. owned three fourths of the company. The Bancrofts' prosperous stationery and bookstores were considered the finest in the state, a reputable firm dealing in high quality merchandise. While business matters were well supervised and no longer needed his attention, H. H. Bancroft became immensely interested in western memorabilia. He began accumulating books and artifacts for his extraordinary personal library. He and his wife went to Europe on book buying trips where they searched for old documents and rare books relating to the history of the western states. With Albert Bancroft supervising the lucrative businesses, they could afford to remain abroad for long periods of time. Despite the Civil War, California merchants prospered due to the use of gold currency while most other states circulated depreciated money.

Bancroft's business outgrew the space in the three-story building and a new site was purchased on Market Street. It was slightly removed from the busy downtown commercial district. A sturdy five-story building was constructed to hold printing presses, engraving and lithograph facilities and a complete bookbinding department. Publishing books became a money making proposition with contracts for supplying textbooks and information about travel, history and religion. The Bancroft publishers consistently produced good, reliable products. One floor in the new building was devoted to H. H. Bancroft's growing collection of historical treasures. Here he stored hundreds of his books, stacks of old newspapers, historic photographs and a variety of documents. He kept adding new items to his collection until he had sixteen thousand volumes of books in his library. He continued to have agents around the world search for any information dealing with western American history and they were authorized to bid on prize collections, often competing with famous museums and galleries.

With an entire floor of working space, Bancroft hired assistants to help index and catalog his tremendous collection. When he realized what a literary treasure he had accumulated, history became a major interest in his life. Bancroft started writing on a grand scale and hired dozens of writers to assist him in portraying the early history of five western states. Teachers, professional writers, newspapermen, librarians and students poured over papers and books in his collection to search for pertinent information. Writers came and went and the office force often referred to the place as a "history factory." Employees copied letters, records, diaries and manuscripts and filed each in appropriate folders. As they continued to organize and index material, Bancroft kept adding to his history collections.

The timing of his collecting was excellent, with many of those involved in California's gold rush still living and quite capable of recalling details of their prospecting days. California's statehood in 1850 was also well remembered by the pioneers whose names and memories were recorded for future generations. Biographical publishing proved to be lucrative with prospective subjects paying as much as $100 per page in advance. Bancroft was also shrewd enough to realize that those whose biographies were included would constitute a sizeable customer list for his books.

In 1881, Bancroft's collection had grown so large that new quarters were necessary once again. Because the five-story business building on Market Street wasn't fireproof, he purchased a lot on the corner of Valencia and Mission streets where a two- story, brick building was erected to house his enormous collection. Iron shutters covered the windows and the building stood alone, not connected to any other structure. Most of Bancroft's assistants worked in the new building indexing and cataloging recent acquisitions. With the resources, time and facilities, the great collector began to publish volumes of books relating to the country's western development. Although he had a devoted wife and five children, gathering, recording and writing history dominated his life.

Bancroft had the habit of writing while standing at his large, revolving, circular desk, often as long as 12 hours a day. Reference material was supplied by his assistants from the vast indexed collection and, if necessary, by hired researchers. In addition to western history, he also wrote of prominent men and their part in the evolution of big business. He printed brochures, advertised in newspapers and hired an army of salesmen to promote book sales through advanced subscriptions.

By 1905, the 73 year-old businessman sought a permanent home for his library that would become available to students and researchers alike. In spite of opposition from academic historians who claimed some historic inaccuracies, the University of California subsequently purchased the Bancroft collection for far less than its appraised value. Just before the material was to be removed to its new home on the Berkeley campus, the devastating 1906 earthquake struck the San Francisco area. Fortunately the sturdy brick building withstood any damage and the collection ultimately found its home in the appropriately named Bancroft Library on campus. It remains as a memorial to his dedication to western history and a priceless heritage for future generations.

Chapter 7

JOSEPH PULITZER
1847-1911

During the winter of 1887, Joseph Pulitzer's eyesight diminished drastically and his New York doctor prescribed a six-month rest in California. He was told not to read, nor write and thus he hired a male secretary to accompany him west in his private Pullman car, the *Newport*. Even though he came to California as a health seeker and to experience a milder winter climate, he could not escape controlling his eastern chain of newspapers. He was a compulsive worker, a perfectionist who revolutionized New York journalism. Despite his prescribed vacation, he kept in communication with his newspaper editors and managers after he left for California on January 14, 1888.

After a brief visit to the posh Hotel Del Monte in Monterey, Pulitzer and his secretary arrived in Riverside on February 20th. They occupied the finest apartment in the Glenwood Hotel and the Miller family provided the best service possible to their distinguished guest. He suffered from a number of ailments resulting from overwork and stressful business negotiations. He had spent most of his life in New York where he worked long hours trying to outmaneuver competing newspapers. Pulitzer had experienced nervous attacks for years and with his failing eyesight, he had become depressed. When he settled in the Glenwood, he discovered the quiet, peaceful atmosphere so relaxing he decided to stay three extra days.

While visiting the Glenwood, he renewed his acquaintance with Albert S. White, a permanent resident of the hotel. White had been an important New York businessman before moving to Riverside in 1882 and the two men had lots to talk about. Pulitzer was introduced to two other men at the hotel, Christopher Columbus Miller and Captain Byron Schermerhorn. These men had served in the Union Army during the Civil War and welcomed Joseph Pulitzer as a fellow veteran.

Riverside officials were anxious to show the New York tycoon around town but the February weather was brisk with snow on surrounding mountains. Joseph Pulitzer nevertheless wanted to see the community and was driven down Magnolia Avenue. At the time, the navel orange crop was ready to harvest and the distinguished guest asked if he could pick an orange to eat. He methodically removed a big orange, slowly peeled it and consumed it on the spot. Later he claimed it was the highlight of his Riverside vacation. The following day he was taken to the top of Mount Rubidoux to witness the magnificent view and to observe construction of a huge hotel. Near the top of the hill were granite blocks for the foundation of the luxury hotel to be known as *The Rubidoux*. Plans called for a combination of Old English and Swiss architecture featuring tall gables and towers with bay windows. Pulitzer believed the new hotel would become a marvelous resort with its unusual design and hilltop location. Three months later, all work on the project ceased for lack of funds and many years later the massive foundation became a reservoir for the Riverside Water Company.

A *Riverside Press* reporter received permission to interview the great editor and was invited to his apartment in the Glenwood. The celebrated publisher stood six feet tall, with a reddish beard parted down the middle. The reporter found him common looking and friendly, not the intimidating man he expected. The interview began when the wealthy New Yorker was asked his impressions of Riverside. Pulitzer did not hesitate in answering.

"Riverside surpasses any place I have seen in southern California, in fact in the state. I am so impressed with Riverside that I will return next year with my family. I hope to send my nine-year-old son, Ralph, because he suffers with asthma and this climate would do him good."

The reporter pointed out that Riverside was a temperance settlement and asked the world traveler his views on prohibition. Pulitzer had definite opinions about that issue.

"Evils accrue from too much indulgence in whisky. I am at a loss to understand any town in California favoring prohibition laws when the wine industry is as great as it is in this state. Your wine is liked. Riverside is destined to be a great resort and nine-tenths of the traveling public drink liquor. Will not extreme prohibition work a hardship to your guests? I am speaking as a traveler now. Claret and light wines hurt no one. Temperance fanaticism will work a detriment to your town. It will hurt and hurt badly."

Future visitors to the Glenwood, Frances Willard, Susan B. Anthony and Carrie Nation would challenge Pulitzer's views on prohibition and adamantly dispute his theories that wine could hurt no one. Regardless of Pulitzer's ideas and opinions, Frank Miller strongly opposed the use of both spirits and tobacco.

While Pulitzer was a guest at the Glenwood, an unusual celestial occurrence took place and frightened many people. An immense light ring encircled the moon and remained in place for hours. One guest at the hotel commented, "It is like everything else in Riverside – the biggest thing I ever saw." Before Joseph Pulitzer left town to join his family in Los Angeles, he ordered three crates of navel oranges to be sent east to his editorial staff at the *New York World*. After he left Riverside, the *Riverside Press* stated:

"Joseph Pulitzer is a fine gentleman of good judgment and concern. He says Riverside is the finest place in California. A man of Mr. Pulitzer's ability should own the world."

In April 1888, Pulitzer returned to New York to resume his hectic routine of work and worry. Even as a child he had fretted about details of everyday life. When he was 17 he left Budapest and came to the United States. He arrived during the Civil War and joined the Union army. In 1868, after the war, he began his newspaper career as a reporter for a German language paper in St. Louis, Missouri where he gained a following of loyal readers. He subsequently became a special correspondent for the *New York Sun* and in 1877 returned to St. Louis to marry beautiful Kate Davis. When he had the opportunity in 1879, Pulitzer purchased the *St. Louis Dispatch* and the *Evening Post* and combined them into the *Post Dispatch*. Within four years this newspaper made him a fortune and an outstanding reputation as a first rate publisher.

In 1883, the 36-year-old Pulitzer acquired the *New York World* and changed its format to be more appealing to working class people. He entered politics, was elected to the House of Representatives from New York and served two years. Newspaper work dominated his life, however, and he continued to write inspiring articles about the rights of working people, children and immigrants. The paper launched crusades against long accepted graft by public officials and set out to clean up the city. In order to educate readers, his newspapers ran stories on self-improvement, proper manners and domestic interests.

When the people of France presented the Statue of Liberty to the people of the United States as a symbol of friendship, the *World* newspaper began a campaign to raise money for a decent pedestal. In 1885, Americans donated pennies, nickels and dimes to pay for the $260,000 base advocated by Pulitzer's paper. The Hungarian immigrant successfully influenced a large audience, realized the power of the press and devoted his time and energy to his work. He never ceased to worry about business and these distressing anxieties led to spells of depression, insomnia and exhaustion.

In 1895, William Randolph Hearst entered the newspaper business with the backing of a huge fortune. He owned the *New York Journal*, a paper in direct competition with Pulitzer's *New York World*. A war of egos developed between owners and the two became fierce opponents. In an effort to sell the most newspapers, their stories were often distorted and did not consistently reflect the truth. Both men were openly accused of yellow journalism. Nonetheless, Joseph Pulitzer strongly believed in competition and relished the idea of outsmarting his adversary.

The astute businessman watched the dynasties of the Vanderbilts and Goulds disappear as younger generations dissipated or lost their family holdings. With this thought in mind, he began tutoring his 11 year-old son Herbert to take control of his newspapers when he died. The last ten years of Pulitzer's life were devoted to plans for the future of his newspaper empire and how best to distribute his vast wealth.

At the age of 56, he donated one million dollars to establish the Columbia University Graduate School of Journalism. In 1903 journalism was not considered a true profession and he attempted to refine this type of writing to a literary standard. There were no ethics or standards of decency and sensationalism and vulgarity regularly appeared in print. It was common practice to run stories, true or untrue, about the personal lives of elected officials. Doctors and lawyers could lose their practice due to articles that questioned their character. Each publisher wrote his cwn editorials and criticized other publishers and correspondents for their views and opinions. Joseph Pulitzer realized the value of a formal education in the field of journalism and he encouraged writers, cartoonists, and photographers to do their very best work and donated prize money for annual competitions.

He died in 1911 and bequeathed half a million dollars each to the New York Philharmonic Society and to the Metropolitan Museum of Art.

He left another million dollars to the Columbia University Graduate School of Journalism plus a large endowment fund to encourage the arts. This provided resources for annual awards known as Pulitzer Prizes, selected for outstanding accomplishments in the fields of journalism, literature, music and art. The Trustees of Columbia University select winners, with recommendations from an advisory board of the journalism school. Categories range from distinguished public service by an American newspaper, editorial writing and quality cartoonist's work of public importance. Other awards are given for outstanding news photography and exceptional reporting of national and international affairs.

The Pulitzer Prizes also encompass books of fiction, history, biography and autobiography. Traveling scholarships are awarded to promising journalists enabling them to study abroad for one year enabling promising students and artisans to continue their education.

The Pulitzer Prizes are prestigious awards that were made possible by a brilliant immigrant who was a perfectionist and idealist.

Chapter 8

RAY LYMAN WILBUR
1875-1949

In 1929 Herbert Hoover became president of the United States and appointed Ray Lyman Wilbur his Secretary of the Interior. These men met when they were students at Stanford University and became lifelong friends. Each had achieved prominence in his specific endeavor. Wilbur's varied careers encompassed the fields of medicine, teaching and administrative work in the university and federal government service. Although he held high ranking positions with great responsibilities, Ray Lyman Wilbur never lost sight of his modest Riverside background where he received his early schooling.

On June 24, 1892 Ray Wilbur graduated from the Riverside High School with Professor C. H. Keyes, Superintendent of Schools, presenting eight diplomas at the commencement exercises in the Loring Opera House. Each of the three girls and five boys participated in the program reading poetry or playing a musical instrument. Ray Wilbur however read a serious essay he had written entitled "Vindication of Shylock" concerning Jewish people and their inhuman treatment at the hands of others through the centuries. At the conclusion of the exercises graduating students and their families were cordially invited to a testimonial dinner at the Glenwood Hotel. In addition to honoring the graduates, the occasion marked the departure of Professor Keyes who was leaving Riverside to become president of the prestigious Throop University.

Attending the dinner party was Ray Wilbur's father, Dwight, a respected member of Riverside's school board. The family was proud of Ray's accomplishments and his parents endeavored to provide a good education for their six children. Because of Ray's good grades and test scores, the family encouraged him to apply to Stanford, a new institution in Palo Alto, California. The university had been named in honor of 15-year-old Leland Stanford Jr. who had died in 1884. The founding president, David Starr Jordan, visited Riverside frequently to recruit students for the new school that opened in 1887. Riverside High School graduates were eligible to enter Harvard, Yale and all California colleges because the school required courses in English, German, Latin, Greek, math and natural sciences and was accredited by the State of California.

Members of the Wilbur family contributed to Ray's first year at Stanford. The nation was then experiencing the first signs of an impending depression and money was not plentiful in his large household. Earlier, in 1887, Dwight Wilbur had moved his family from Iowa to Riverside where he purchased a small citrus grove and, in order to supplement his fluctuating farm income, worked as a real estate agent. He bought property on a hill overlooking Linden Street and built a yellow brick house for his large family. Many years later the site became the location of a reservoir.

The Wilbur family attended the First Congregational Church and befriended members Frank and Isabella Miller. Church socials, holiday celebrations and family gatherings brought the congregation together for many good times. The Wilbur house was filled with books dealing with the classics, scientific information and religious teachings. Young Ray, an awkward country boy, became interested in the wonders of nature. Living east of downtown, he often walked in the hills surrounding Sycamore Canyon and collected bird eggs and insects. He learned to identify and classify his specimens and this curiosity about nature may have influenced him to seek a medical career. His subsequent educational achievements included his medical degree following studies in Germany, England and in New England. At the age of 36, Dr. Ray Lyman Wilbur became dean of Stanford's Medical School.

In 1916, Dr. Wilbur gave up his medical career to become president of Leland Stanford University. This prestigious position attained by a Riversider made big news in local newspapers. The *Riverside Daily Press* stated, "The distinction which has fallen to Dr. Wilbur is considered by his many friends here as distinction for Riverside where he lived as a boy and young man and received his early schooling." In addition to local acclaim and praise, Stanford graduates throughout the nation were delighted to have an alumnus appointed president of their alma mater. Dr. David Starr Jordan had formulated successful policies and curriculum of the university and a former student carried on the work.

Even though Dr. Wilbur was a busy man, he visited Riverside frequently and kept in close touch with his brothers and sisters scattered throughout the nation. His siblings were dynamic achievers celebrated within their own fields of expertise. Curtis, his older brother, was an

Annapolis graduate and served as Secretary of the Navy in President Calvin Coolidge's cabinet. Later, he became Chief Justice of the California Supreme Court. Ray Wilbur's sisters were involved in social work and missionary pursuits, many under the auspices of the Congregational church. One sister became an executive in the Young Woman's Christian Association and members of the Wilbur family were well known for their humanitarian work.

Whenever Ray Wilbur came to Riverside, he visited Frank Miller. The men admired each others achievements and their friendship endured throughout their lives. On Frank Miller's Mission Inn office wall a photograph of Ray Wilbur was proudly displayed next to other notable friends and acquaintances. In April 1922, Dr. Wilbur came to Riverside to address local doctors, city officials and the public about the need for a new hospital. The forum took place in the Music Room of the Mission Inn, filled with civic-minded citizens. The town's only hospital had burned and Dr. Wilbur stressed the importance of constructing a new building, centrally located to serve all citizens of the community. The old hospital built in 1905 had sustained serious fire damage to the top two floors and patients had been transferred temporarily to the March Field hospital. A spectator commented religious groups often travel to Asia and Africa to build hospitals yet Riverside badly needed a new facility. Consequently, Dr. Wilbur endorsed the pressing need for a new building to be constructed as soon as possible. His enthusiasm sparked the beginning of a campaign to raise money for the project. Frank Miller donated $25,000 to the building fund and townspeople followed suit. School children gave nickels and dimes to the drive and in 1924 a new community hospital opened at the corner of Magnolia Avenue and Fourteenth Street.

When President Hoover appointed Dr. Ray Lyman Wilbur his Interior Secretary, Wilbur took a leave of absence from Stanford and moved to Washington, D.C. He became involved in national matters concerning Indian affairs, conservation of natural resources and other diverse problems. Nevertheless, the six foot tall, lean man, who incidentally resembled Abraham Lincoln, remained calm under fire and honorably fulfilled his cabinet post from 1929 to 1933. During this period he directed construction of what was originally called Boulder Dam, considered the greatest conservation project of the century. When Herbert Hoover was Secretary of Commerce under President Harding in 1922, he visited the recommended site for the dam. As chairman of the Colorado River Commission, Hoover's engineering background was invaluable and qualified him for the job of determining the dam's location. Hoover and Wilbur combined their efforts to complete the Colorado River dam known today as Hoover Dam.

During his term in Washington, Wilbur also fought for the preservation of the National Park Service. He served on many different committees and boards of directors with dignity and agility and was considered a respected government official. The family lived in a Washington hotel, a common practice for appointed officials. He had married Marguerite Blake in 1898 while a medical student, and their six children were now grown. When they were in Washington, Wilbur's hometown friends and neighbors followed his political career with great interest. In addition they kept in touch with other local high school graduates who had also achieved distinction in their chosen fields. The most popular personality was Marcella Craft and her famous international operatic career. They knew of her gala performances before European royalty, her outstanding voice and daring costumes. Another graduate, Dane Coolidge became a famous writer and Edmund Heller a world-renowned naturalist. The celebrated status of other graduates notwithstanding, the 1930 edition of the local high school yearbook, *The Orange and Green*, was dedicated to Dr. Ray Lyman Wilbur, an honor he graciously accepted.

In the spring of 1933, Dr. Wilbur and his family returned to Stanford where he served as president until his retirement in 1943. On March 25, 1936, Wilbur and a party of friends were on their way to Palm Springs after visiting Hoover Dam and decided to spend the night at the Mission Inn. Driving from the dam to Riverside the travelers experienced a serious snow and hailstorm, an unusual occurrence for March. Frank Miller had died the year before but his sister, Alice Richardson, and his daughter, Allis Hutchings, made him feel welcome. The Wilbur party mingled with other guests and there was much discussion about a new assistant football coach at Stanford. Dr. Wilbur commented he was highly pleased with the signing of Bobby Grayson.

"Grayson is a popular fellow with the student body and gets along well with the boys. He proved himself a great grid star and should be a successful coach."

When the Wilbur party left the Mission Inn for Palm Springs they took the Pines-to-Palms highway, a scenic drive through mountains and desert. The following year, 1937, Ray Wilbur co-authored a definitive book entitled, *The Hoover Policies* published by Charles Scribner & Company. This same year his brother, Federal Judge Curtis D. Wilbur of San Francisco, came to Riverside for his son's wedding and this occasion resulted in a family reunion. The happy couple was married in the Mission Inn on March 24, 1937, with the extended Wilbur family in attendance.

Sixty-five year old Ray Wilbur reached his retirement age in 1940 but due to Pearl Harbor and the ensuing war, he remained president of the university until 1943. The tall, gentleman always claimed that he had two homes, one in Palo Alto and his yellow brick house in Riverside. The Wilburs were one of Riverside's most famous families known for their achievements and many accomplishments.

While Ray Lyman Wilbur was still a student at Stanford University, a controversial woman named Susan B. Anthony visited the Glenwood Hotel.

Chapter 9

SUSAN B. ANTHONY
1820-1906

Susan B. Anthony was one of six children born to a tightly bonded Quaker family in Massachusetts. Although named Susan Brownell Anthony, she chose not to use her middle name, just the initial B. Educated in a Quaker boarding school, she turned to teaching to make a living, one of the few professions available to women. In lieu of marriage she felt the need to become self-supporting because her father's untimely bankruptcy had left the family nearly penniless. She believed marriage without equality inconceivable and accordingly never married. Ultimately she became headmistress of a New York girl's school where she refined her leadership qualities.

Miss Anthony gave up her teaching career and devoted her life to campaigning for women's rights. At the time, many women schooled themselves in reform issues and became dedicated to social changes. The former schoolteacher was often ridiculed and ostracized for her controversial views and outspoken opinions. The name Susan B. Anthony became associated throughout the country with the crusade for rights of women. She kept a full schedule as an ardent speaker, organizer and writer.

In 1895, Susan B. Anthony accepted an invitation to speak to the Women's Congress Auxiliary at the California Midwinter Exposition in San Francisco. The 75-year-old activist asked if her good friend Reverend Anna Howard Shaw could accompany her to share some of the scheduled speaking engagements. When newspapers reported that Miss Anthony and Reverend Shaw were to visit California, dozens of invitations and cash donations were received from old friends and distant relatives. The money paid the ladies travel and hotel expenses when they were not guests in private homes. Their extensive itinerary included an overnight stay at the Glenwood as guests of the Frank Miller family.

The women headed west on April 27, 1895, and appeared in Chicago, St. Louis, Denver and Salt Lake City. Anna Shaw preached in the Mormon Tabernacle and her messages dealing with women's rights were accepted with enthusiasm. Miss Anthony met Mrs. Leland Stanford who was then in Salt Lake and the women had a pleasant afternoon discussing women's rights and the growing temperance movement, Mrs. Stanford made a generous donation to help the two dedicated crusaders. In Reno, Nevada, the suffragists addressed college students and received high praise. Receptions were held in their honor and they received flowers and tributes to celebrate their good work.

Newspapers announced the women's schedule in advance to ensure an enthusiastic crowd. On May 20, they were in San Francisco in time for the opening of the Women's Congress where Susan B. Anthony received a loud round of applause for her selfless devotion to the suffrage movement. Some people attended her well-publicized lecture to see the stern, plain, unmarried woman who had become America's outspoken champion of women's rights.

There were common goals in both suffrage and temperance movements and each shared some of the same leaders. Susan B. Anthony advocated women's rights and worked for equality of all women. The Women's Christian Temperance Union, headed by Frances Willard, became a worldwide organization devoted to prohibition of alcohol. Carrie Nation's methods of destroying saloons made bold headlines but few activists condoned her strategy.

Susan B. Anthony maintained laws were unjust to women with men legislating for everyone. She believed women should have equal power, and share responsibilities of lawmaking. She adamantly expressed her disapproval of the theory that women might be influenced by their emotions and lacked judicial experience.

Miss Anthony frequently quoted Abraham Lincoln when he stated, "No man is good enough to govern another man without his consent." She would quickly add, "No man is good enough to govern any woman without her consent." This statement usually brought a reaction from the audience and women waved their white handkerchiefs as a signal of approval.

Since this small, Quaker woman received little payment for most of her lectures, she depended on gifts and donations to support her work for equal rights. She wore a plain, black silk or satin dress in public, a yearly gift from a good friend. On occasion she appeared in a black, ministerial type robe with a white collar at the neck and wrists. Her colorless hair parted down the middle was severely combed over her ears and coiled low in the back. Although normally dressed in a simple Quaker manner, she deviated from tradition on her first trip to California when she visited Yosemite. In 1895, after a busy day at the San Francisco convention, Miss Anthony and Reverend Shaw were treated to an enjoyable rest and sightseeing trip in Yosemite.

The two ladies were impressed with the panoramic view of the steep mountains and the pristine beauty of Yosemite. Susan B. Anthony went horseback riding, hiked among tall tress and marched through the valley dressed in the new fashionable outfit known as bloomers. This eccentric costume consisted of full pantaloons to the ankles with a short skirt gathered below the knees. The quiet serenity of the area deeply impressed the women and they experienced a religious awakening. Anna Shaw had the privilege of naming a tree in the Mariposa Grove the Susan B. Anthony Tree. It stood near trees named for George Washington and Abraham Lincoln. After several delightful days, the women headed south to Los Angeles.

On June 12, 1895, the two women addressed a Los Angeles audience and continued challenging the male population to give females equal rights. The following day the ladies arrived in Riverside as guests of the Glenwood Hotel. Susan B. Anthony was related to Frank W. Richardson, co-manager of the Glenwood with his wife Alice Miller Richardson. Miss Anthony's maternal grandmother was Susannah Richardson, linking their families in past generations. The Frank Richardsons were delighted to entertain such distinguished visitors and arranged a successful reception in the parlor of the Glenwood.

Alice and Frank Richardson took the ladies for a pleasant carriage ride around Riverside and drove down scenic Magnolia Avenue. The eastern ladies picked a ripe orange from a tree, peeled and ate it on the spot. This new experience was the highlight of their visit and the pleasure of picking and eating a fresh orange was talked about for sometime. After their tour, the ladies relaxed in the quiet, garden atmosphere of the hotel before their evening lecture in the Loring Opera House. That evening, Elmer W. Holmes, a former local newspaper publisher and assemblyman, agreed to be the program chairman. In spite of his participation, he made it known he didn't wish to be associated with the women's rights platform and was merely presiding over the meeting as a courtesy. Miss Anthony was the first to speak and in her dignified manner she related a few advancements made by women.

"Fifty years ago it was not thought proper for a woman to have an opinion, much less express it. For every right now possessed by women, someone had to fight a battle. Finally, women are allowed to write for newspapers and magazines."

Reverend Anna Shaw also proved to be a good speaker with a sense of humor when talking about political equality for women. This interesting lady was educated as a medical doctor before she studied for the ministry and became the first woman ordained to preach in the Methodist Church. Both Miss Anthony and Miss Shaw possessed great physical vigor along with the remarkable ability to inspire their audiences. Each had a single-minded devotion to winning suffrage for women that was endorsed by local members of the Women's Christian Temperance Union. Occasionally, their appeals reached some progressive men.

The two women continued their scheduled appearances and traveled to San Diego and surrounding towns before returning to their homes in New York. The following year, 1896, both ladies returned to California to attend another convention in San Francisco. The primary purpose of this trip was to lobby male voters in California to vote for the passage of an amendment giving women in the state the right to vote. Susan B. Anthony was an honored guest as she sat in the center of the stage in a chair draped in pink and red roses. In spite of the fact that this woman had once been the most ridiculed person in the nation, she now was deemed an effective political force. Despite her influence, however, the California amendment did not pass.

Once again the notable women were entertained and honored with many social affairs and parties. A most memorable occasion occurred when they were invited to the home of Mr. and Mrs. William Keith in Berkeley. The noted artist, William Keith, presented Miss Anthony one of his extraordinary paintings of Yosemite. The artist had toured the Sierra Nevada Mountains for many years and his impressive paintings reflected the majestic colors and details of the beautiful scenery. Miss Anthony treasured this painting and displayed it over the mantel in her Rochester home she shared with her sister Mary. The old brick house contained simple furniture and family pictures befitting two Quaker ladies.

In July 1897, the Adams, Anthony, Lapham and Richardson families held a reunion in New England but Frank Richardson of Riverside did not attend. Business kept him from leaving town. He spent most of his time managing the Glenwood for his brother-in-law, Frank Miller, who was busy planning a new hotel. Miller offered the Board of Supervisors a proposition whereby he would erect a suitable building for a courthouse in conjunction with his new hotel. The proposition was accepted and the Supervisors approved the floor plans. Frank Miller tried to raise money to finance the building but failed to obtain the necessary support. Later, in 1903, the new Glenwood Mission Inn and the Riverside County Courthouse, located on Tenth Street, were completed and each has become an important city landmark

In March 1906, Susan B. Anthony died of pneumonia. Six months later, her cousin Frank W. Richardson also died. Fourteen years after Miss Anthony's death, the 19th amendment to the Constitution passed giving women the right to vote. After 40 years of trying to pass such an amendment, it was adopted in 1920 and appropriately named "The Anthony Amendment."

Women were not the only citizens that were denied the right to vote at the turn of the century. In 1900 the United States adopted the Territory of Hawaii and Hawaiians became citizens but could not vote in a national election. Sanford Dole was then Governor of the Hawaiian Islands.

Chapter 10

SANFORD BALLARD DOLE
1844-1926

In February 1898, Riverside's Chamber of Commerce held a public reception in the Glenwood Hotel for President of the Hawaiian Republic Sanford Dole and his wife Anna. American and Hawaiian flags decorated the parlors filled with bright flowers and greenery. Hundreds of people attended the informal gathering anxious to meet the Doles or to renew old acquaintances. Many townspeople had previously met the distinguished gentleman in 1890 when he visited his brother George, a respected Riverside businessman and citrus grower.

The Dole brothers, George and Sanford, were born in Hawaii where their father Reverend Daniel Dole established a missionary school. The school opened in 1842 in a small building made of adobe walls and thatched roof. Many years later, the school became the celebrated Oahu College. Education was a motivating factor in the Dole family and after completing their Hawaiian education the brothers traveled to the United States to pursue higher academic interests. While George, the older of the two, studied sugar cane production in the southern states, Sanford attended Williams College in Massachusetts. After completing their advanced studies, the brothers returned to their home in the Islands. Sanford had studied international law and in 1869, after passing the bar examination, began his law practice. That same year he married Anna Cate of Maine, also a child of missionaries. As a young lawyer, he became interested in politics and in 1887 was appointed a judge. Sanford Dole knew most of the important people in Hawaii and everyone knew Judge Dole. Furthermore, he was highly regarded by his political opponents as a fair and honest gentleman.

That same year, prominent Hawaiian banker Charles Reed Bishop came to the mainland for pleasure and leisurely traveled throughout southern California. He had lived in the Islands for 40 years, married a cousin of King Lunalilo and was also a member of the House of Lords in the Hawaiian legislature and council to King Kalakaua. His banking firm of Bishop & Company was well known throughout the financial world. On October 19, 1887, the distinguished visitor arrived in Riverside and spent the night at the Glenwood Hotel. While touring Riverside he observed large quantities of grapes then drying in trays, soon to become fancy packed raisins and distributed to world markets. He was also impressed with hundreds of acres of navel orange trees then loaded with maturing fruit. When he returned to Hawaii, he spoke of the remarkable town of Riverside with its production of diverse crops. George and Sanford Dole no doubt heard banker Bishop's discussions about the town and the prosperous future of the area.

In 1869 George Dole had married the daughter of a New England missionary and settled on a Hawaiian plantation and farmed sugar cane. Due to problems with labor and trade agreements, he changed his occupation to teaching school in Honolulu where his children could also obtain a better education. Clara and George Dole had 12 children and the family lived a healthy, Hawaiian outdoor lifestyle. In spite of their good environment, the parents felt the need for better schools and universities that were available on the mainland. Furthermore, the unstable Hawaiian monarchy caused concern and in 1889 George Dole moved his family to Riverside, California. He had previously considered the possibility of a move to the community described so eloquently by Charles Bishop. He found the town an ideal place where his children could receive a good education while he could pursue his agricultural interests and provide for his large family.

He purchased a 20-acre ranch on Arlington Avenue near Magnolia that included an existing two story Victorian house. With two boys away at college, there were still ten children at home and a baby on the way. In October George wrote to his brother that he had dried and sold nearly nine tons of raisins from his ranch. He added that the family was looking forward to his visit and asked him to bring seeds for his Riverside garden. The George Doles had been in their new home for a year when his brother Sanford and wife paid them a visit. They spent the Christmas holidays in Riverside. Six-foot tall Judge Sanford Dole had a long, pointed bushy beard that gave him a most distinguished appearance. He dressed in immaculate white suits that were appropriate for tropical climates but not considered customary winter apparel in California. As a leading citizen in Hawaiian politics, he had joined others in considering an alliance with the United States and a possible annexation.Under Queen Liliuokalani's reign, there were some Hawaiians who wished to keep the monarchy, while others favored a British rule. Continuing anxiety about Hawaii's future prompted Sanford Dole, with no children of his own, to write regularly to his Riverside nieces and nephews informing them of political changes. He endeavored to keep his brother's children mindful of their honorable Hawaiian heritage.

The Doles lived in a big, comfortable house in Honolulu hidden from the street by a row of royal palm trees. In the entry hung a huge American flag and the rooms were filled with inviting lounging chairs. Tables held books and magazines with fine paintings and works of art were displayed throughout the comfortable house. Open doors led into beautifully landscaped gardens.

Political tensions in Hawaii erupted in 1893 and the Queen subsequently relinquished her rule to a provisional government. Sanford Dole was chosen President of the provisional government and worked with legislators to draft a constitution modeled after that of the United States. Working towards the process of annexation to the United States, the Republic of Hawaii was created July 4, 1894. The Cleveland administration opposed annexation but President Sanford Dole nevertheless, signed the Treaty of Annexation and waited for its ratification by the United States Senate. After numerous delays, Dole was urged to go to Washington and confer with William McKinley, the newly elected president, and to lobby for Hawaii's annexation. While Mrs. Dole was first lady of the Islands, she held open house every Friday afternoon and it became a social custom. Visitors filled the Dole house and discussed local issues with friends and neighbors. Mrs. Dole was an active hostess who made everyone feel welcome.

En route to Washington, D.C. in 1898, President Dole and his supporters arrived in San Francisco and stayed at the Occidental Hotel. In honor of the President's visit, a huge Hawaiian flag flew from the top of the building. The influential San Franciscan Claus Spreckels, head of the sugar trust, was opposed to annexation of the Hawaiian Islands and worked to prevent its ratification. Although this distraction was troubling it did not deter Sanford Dole from visiting his family in Riverside.

Sanford and Anna Dole spent a few delightful days at the George Dole ranch and visited old friends and Riverside acquaintances including Frank Miller. Miller held a special reception in the Glenwood for the Doles and many local citizens greeted the distinguished gentleman in his spotless white suit. President Dole previously had purchased a small Riverside citrus grove in Arlington Heights that his brother managed for him. When he inspected the property, he picked an orange, peeled off the skin and enjoyed eating his own fruit. While the Sanford Doles spent several nights at the Glenwood relaxing, the United States battleship *Maine* exploded in Havana sparking the ensuing Spanish-American war.

Upon arriving in Washington, D. C, President William McKinley held a state dinner in honor of President Dole. Government officials were impressed with the dignified, respected gentleman. President McKinley led Anna Dole into the beautifully decorated stately dining room. She was described as a refined, cultured lady dressed in a sedate black velvet outfit. In contrast to Mrs. Dole's sober colored dress, Ida McKinley wore white satin and was escorted into the dining room by Sanford Dole. The immense table was set for 70 guests and the reception was a great honor for the Doles. Even though everyone appeared congenial, the catastrophe in Havana overshadowed any chance for a happy celebration. The Spanish-American War also eliminated any immediate discussions about Hawaii's future. Several years after the war, in 1900, Dole's mission to Washington proved successful. The Territory of Hawaii was established and Sanford Dole became its first Governor.

During these years of adversity between Hawaii and the United States, informative letters between Sanford Dole in Honolulu and the Riverside Doles continued. George Dole's 13 children all attended college and excelled in both athletic and academic activities. Leland Stanford University had at least one Dole enrolled continuously from 1891 to 1912. In 1899, Charles Dole graduated from Stanford University where he befriended Mrs. Leland Stanford. He returned to Hawaii and became an important attorney and his Uncle Sanford's trusted companion. In 1905 Mrs. Stanford died in Hawaii and Charles Dole helped the family through trying times. Sanford Dole had a New England nephew named James who moved to the Islands around the turn of the century and developed the important pineapple industry.

In 1900 all Hawaiians were made citizens of the United States but had no vote in a national election. A combination of the British and American flags was adopted as the banner of the territory and in 1903 it became the official flag of the Hawaiian Islands. Governor Sanford Dole served as head of state for several years and resigned to become a federal judge.

In February 1911, Judge Dole unveiled a statue of President William McKinley at a Hawaiian high school bearing McKinley's name. After the President's assassination in 1901, Dole began a campaign to raise funds to honor McKinley whom he considered a great friend of the Hawaiian people.

In the spring of 1911, the Sanford Doles decided to take an extended trip to Europe and visit old friends and interesting places they wanted to see. On their way east they stopped in Riverside to visit his brother and family. George Dole's daughter, Dr. Emily Dole, was accompanying them on the six-month journey. The visitors discovered the city had grown and changed since their last trip. The Mission Inn was a grand hotel built around a front courtyard with landscaped grounds.

They left Riverside on April 9, 1911, and leisurely traveled for a month before reaching New York. After an extended European vacation, the Doles returned to Honolulu. In 1916, Judge Dole retired from the bench after years of serving the Hawaiian people.

Riversiders remembered meeting the personable President of Hawaii in the decorated parlor of the Glenwood Hotel and greeting the same man as Governor of Hawaii in the spacious lobby of the Mission Inn.

Chapter 11

GEORGE WHARTON JAMES
1858-1923

On March 12, 1895, hotel guests and townspeople gathered in the Glenwood to hear Dr. George Wharton James expound on the wonders of the Mt. Lowe Railroad. The tall, handsome speaker showed slides on his stereopticon projector and explained how ascending and descending cable cars counter balanced each other on the winding road up the mountain. Open cars traveled the steep grade over trestles and hairpin turns to reach the summit of Echo Mountain in the San Gabriel hills above Pasadena. Photos from that vantage point showed the entire countryside with panoramic views of the valleys and canyons. A large hotel designed to resemble an Alpine Chalet had been built and was opened for business. George James, the ultimate promoter and eager salesman, was the social director of the hilltop hotel. After informing his interested audience of the beauties and amenities to be found at Echo Mountain, he carefully explained how to get there and back in one day.

Dr. James was six-feet tall, a handsome man with a bushy black beard. His pleasing firm voice bore a slight English accent adding to his captivating personality. Born in England, he had been a sickly child and became self-educated and a prolific reader. He developed the ability to retain whatever he read and could easily repeat long, complicated verses word for word. Music was also a part of his early life and he cultivated a melodious singing voice to accompany his skill on the piano and organ.

An ordained Methodist minister, he first came to the United States in 1881 with a group of itinerant evangelists in western Nevada. His wife joined him from England the following year and in 1887 he accepted the pastorate of the Long Beach Methodist Church. A few years later, following her accusations of sexual misconduct, an unpleasant divorce ensued and Reverend James was dismissed. Although he was subsequently cleared of all charges and reinstated in the church, the resultant publicity compelled him to leave southern California.

For the next four years he roamed throughout the southwest exploring the Colorado and Mojave deserts while communing with nature. James lived with various Indian tribes and learned their legends, observed their basket-making and marveled at their intricate weaving techniques. He studied their ideals and traditions and participated in their simple lifestyle. The outdoor environment lifted his spiritual outlook and he found peace and contentment in the vast deserts of Arizona, Utah and Nevada. During these years of living with various tribes, he acquired a priceless knowledge of their lore and customs.

When he returned to southern California in 1895, he embarked on a new career as a lecturer and writer, dropped the title "Reverend" and adopted the use of "Doctor" or "Professor." Thus revitalized, he assumed a professional career at a time when an interest in handmade Indian artifacts was sweeping the country. Beautifully crafted baskets and handwoven rugs were appearing in households across the nation. Collectors, such as Fred Harvey, were buying directly from the artisans and many premium pieces ended up in museum collections. This popular trend ironically brought about a query for more knowledge of handcrafted objects and the craftsmen who produced them. Intricate designs, dyes and methods of creating them became of paramount interest. A number of writers including Dr. James pursued this educational opportunity and contributed informative articles to magazines and periodicals explaining and expounding on the wonders of the southwest and its inhabitants.

With his entrepreneurial eye, Professor James published elaborate travel guides and occasionally conducted tours for the increasing number of eastern travelers. He continually wrote articles praising the wonders of California and his enthusiastic salesmanship paid off in terms of his financial well-being. In spite of his success however, he soon found a formidable competitor in a fellow writer, Charles Fletcher Lummis. Lummis disliked James and resented the former minister for infringing on his dominance of the subject of early southern California culture. In 1901, Lummis alleged that James deceived his readers in a London magazine article wherein he claimed to have witnessed a sacred Navajo dance, not available to non-members of the tribe. In retribution, as editor of a Los Angeles magazine, *Land of Sunshine*, Lummis resurrected the Long Beach scandal and continued his tirade of James until the day he died. He maintained to the end that James pirated the work of others and included known falsehoods to produce his sensational stories. Through it all, however, James remained uncritical of California history writers including Lummis.

Eight months after Professor James first lectured in the parlor of the Glenwood Hotel, he married Emma Farnsworth and settled in a two story, dark shingled home on Raymond Avenue in Pasadena. His Craftsman style house was filled with Indian baskets and hand-woven blankets collected in his travels. There he worked at his walnut, roll-top desk in the library and wrote numerous articles and some 40 books about his adventures with nature and his studies of American Indians. He became an honorary president of the Robert Browning Club of Pasadena and the International New Thought Alliance. A few of his diversified, illustrated books are *Indian Basketry* and *How to Make Indian Baskets, Indians of the Painted Desert,* and *In and Around Grand Canyon.* Most of his informative books became early reference guides for travelers and collectors but a wide variety of readers enjoyed reading about his absorbing adventures.

Because of the increasing interest in Indian baskets, George James organized the Basket Fraternity, a club of basket lovers and collectors headquartered in Pasadena. Annual dues were one dollar and there was but one condition of membership, a fascination for Indian basketry. Its primary goal was to revive the ancient arts and use of native materials for artistic authenticity. Members were encouraged to conduct lecture tours and special collections and traveling libraries were made available on loan to other museums and institutions.

In 1895, Charles Lummis and architect Arthur Benton founded the Landmarks Club, an organization dedicated to the preservation of the California missions. George James and Frank Miller were among its early members. Through his magazine, *Land of Sunshine,* Lummis gained a great deal of literary influence and was instrumental in launching the careers of many writers of the southwest. The magazine subsequently changed its name to *Out West* and when Lummis retired in 1909 to become a Los Angeles City librarian, George Wharton James became editor-in-chief. Although the two men were fierce rivals, they shared many common interests. Both were well-educated, ambitious showmen with intense interests in southwest culture and each had experienced desert living and revitalization of the spirit. As editor, James was no less inspiring than his predecessor as he continued to write of the Spanish influence in California, the southwest Indians and the reclamation of the desert.

Theodore Roosevelt once commented, "James has done more to make the wonders of the Southwest known to the world than any other ten men." The busy lecture schedule of James's increased his popularity and inevitably increased the sale of his books. He mesmerized audiences with his appealing voice, his abundant energy and his good looks. Dressed in formal black frock coats, he depicted the typical professor, a role he successfully emulated. Even though he had some strange habits, such as nude sunbathing and an excessive exercise routine, his compelling personality and his perfect illustrated color slides made him a celebrated and sought after lecturer.

James expanded his sphere of influence when he contributed several volumes to a series of books advertised as *See America First*. These books covered North America including Canada and Alaska. James wrote, *California: Romantic and Beautiful; New Mexico: the Land of Delight Makers;* and *Arizona; the Wonderland.* All three had decorative hard covers, beautiful illustrations and cost six dollars each.

On Christmas Eve 1909, Frank Miller invited Professor James to give an illustrated lecture to Mission Inn hotel guests. Since the Cloister Wing was not completely finished, guests gathered in the expansive lobby. Part of the new wing included the Music Room, a picturesque room capable of accommodating large gatherings. The assembled guests attentively listened to Dr. James speak on "Ramona Country and the California Missions." A program of holiday music followed his short Christmas Eve talk. The Mission Inn management then entertained their employees and their families with a special holiday dinner, a tradition started by Frank Miller some years before. This year, however, artisans employed in the construction crew of the Cloister Wing were included. There were 140 dinner guests, including George James and his wife, who enjoyed the hospitality of the Mission Inn and Frank Miller.

The self-proclaimed professor was a frequent guest at the Mission Inn. He admired Frank Miller's concern for California's Indians and for sponsoring the first Indian Conference on the west coast in 1908. Whenever Miller was in need of a guest speaker to entertain special guests, George James was always available. One of his last visits to Riverside occurred in October 1922 when he came to the Mission Inn to introduce a prominent Sioux woman, a descendant of Sitting Bull. Mrs. Gertrude Honnin was nationally known for her keen interest in the problems of her people. An attentive audience filled the Music Room when 64-year-old Professor James introduced the speaker. Local citizens would remember his last visit when the following year he died of pneumonia in a Seventh-Day Adventist Sanitarium in Napa County. Decades of lecturing and writing about the healthy, productive life styles of American Indians had taken its toll. It was stated he died of exhaustion and overwork.

Chapter 12

MADAME HELENA MODJESKA
1844-1909

Charming Madame Modjeska passed through the doors of the Mission Inn many times during her appearances at the Loring Opera House. Riversiders admired the romantic Bohemian lifestyle of the Polish actress and were intrigued with her sentimental European background. She had left her beloved Poland in protest of a new political regime but remained loyal to her homeland. Ironically, her early years were filled with both success and sorrow.

When Helena was 17, she made her Polish debut as an actress and soon became a leading lady. In 1861, she married Gustav Modrzejewske and four years later he died leaving her with a son, Ralph. She later married Count Chlapowski and legally shortened her stage name to Modjeska. As a star in the Russian Imperial Theater and an illustrious Shakespearean actress she was known for her talents and beauty. Modjeska became famous throughout Europe, gained enormous popularity and a large number of followers. Her opinions and criticism of Russian control over Poland eventually made life difficult for the family and they sought political freedom in America.

In 1876 they settled in a small agricultural community in southern California where German and Polish emigrants had founded the town of Anaheim. Later, Modjeska and family acquired a 665-acre ranch nearby in Santiago Canyon and commissioned famous New York architect Stanford White to design a country style home. The two-story gabled house, built in 1888, blended with the natural landscape and was named *Arden* after the enchanted forest in Shakespeare's *As You Find It*.

After Modjeska improved her English pronunciation, the Count encouraged her to resume her acting career. He became her manager and she first performed in San Francisco and found immediate success. Within a short time, she was the brightest star on the West Coast. Due to her flamboyant personality, attractive appearance and flawless acting, audiences were eager to see her perform and she gained a devoted following. As her popularity increased, eastern theaters became interested in her acting ability. She accepted invitations to appear in Boston and New

York where she received rave reviews. Her beautiful clear voice and passionate acting drew many reluctant spectators to legitimate opera houses and theaters to witness her magnificent talents. Modjeska and the Count enjoyed America's high society and friendships with theatrical celebrities.

In eastern engagements she was co-starred with handsome actor Maurice Barrymore. The striking couple played Shakespearean roles, often so realistic and passionate that audiences wondered if they were indeed acting. The celebrated Modjeska-Barrymore troupe took their plays on the road in the fall of 1882 and the families traveled in luxurious Palace Pullman cars. Modjeska's private car, named *The Poland,* contained all the comforts of home. The salon and sleeping rooms were elegantly furnished with fine upholstered chairs and paintings covered the walls. Each day large vases of fresh flowers were placed in the cars.

Modjeska entertained selected members of the cast in keeping with protocol that existed in the American theater. Touring cast members lived in less pretentious quarters and seldom mingled socially with the stars of the show. Modjeska's Polish chef prepared delectable dishes native to her homeland and gloved waiters served the lavish meals. Although the Barrymore family had their own luxury car, they often had their meals in *The Poland.* The hospitable actress developed a strong attachment to the Barrymore children, especially little Ethel who reminded her of the infant daughter she had lost.

Modjeska's reputation was well established by 1893 when the Chicago World's Fair opened. When she appeared there, the striking actress wore a brilliant red and white dress to signify Poland's national colors. On top of her full head of shiny, black hair rested a diamond crown and her regal actions resembled those of royalty. Regardless of this courtly display, Modjeska was an unwelcome guest in her native land because of her outspoken criticism and anti-Russian speeches. In America, however, she was well received and enjoyed special privileges and acknowledgments. In spite of her extraordinary prestige, a younger, vibrant French actress, Sarah Bernhardt challenged Modjeska's dominance on the American stage when she began to tour the country.

The family home in Santiago Canyon became a welcome refuge for the couple after long months of traveling from one engagement to another. The large, rambling house overlooked a small lake and the hilly property offered a degree of privacy. Old oak trees shaded the house that was surrounded by grapevines and citrus trees. The ranch, tended by hired help, continued to expand until it covered nearly 14,000 acres. Most of the property consisted of wilderness and remained in its natural state. Modjeska and the Count enjoyed entertaining and the house was often filled with friends and neighbors. Local ranchers were good friends, especially James Irvine Jr., heir to the extensive Irvine Ranch in Orange County. James and Frances Irvine had three children and they named their only daughter Helena for Helena Modjeska.

At the age of 60, the great actress made certain changes to her lifestyle. In 1905, she sold her treasured Orange County estate to a Mr. Moss of Chicago for $30,000. She decided to retire from the stage and planned her yearlong farewell tour of the United States. When she reached Riverside, it was not the first time she had appeared in the Loring Opera House. In 1899, she had played *Lady Macbeth* to a captivated audience and had accepted Frank Miller's hospitality as his guest in the Glenwood Hotel.

On the stormy evening of February 12, 1906, Madame Helena Modjeska made her final appearance in the Loring appearing in the play *Mary Stuart*. Because the date marked Abraham Lincoln's birthday, a patriotic spirit prevailed throughout the theater generously decorated with countless flags. Displayed in the spacious foyer was a large picture of Lincoln perfectly draped in shimmering silk American flags. Inside a radiant Polish flag was suspended from the high opera house balcony with American flags hanging on either side.

When the orchestra played the "Star Spangled Banner" the huge stage curtain slowly rose to reveal a gigantic American flag and the unexpected scene inspired enthusiastic applause. The audience became subdued when Madame Modjeska magically appeared on stage and as she portrayed her dramatic role, she held the attention of her audience during scene after scene. Although her acting was considered artistic and dignified, some critics felt her performance was not up to the high standards of previous years. Even at age 62 she remained beautiful with flashing eyes and a pretty face. When the curtain fell after the third act, a standing ovation greeted the retiring actress. Resounding applause saluted each curtain call as the heavy stage curtain rose and fell with every encore. Magnificent bouquets and heaping baskets of fruit were passed over the footlights to be placed at her feet when she could no longer hold the tributes.

Frank Miller made an unexpected appearance on stage and his impromptu presence confused the audience. With gentle but firm actions he carefully draped the folds of a spectacular Polish flag around the shoulders of Madame Modjeska. A guest at the Mission Inn, Mrs. Francis Bacon of Boston and a friend of the actress, had handmade the flag when a Polish flag could not be located in Riverside. Tears filled Modjeska's eyes as strains of Poland's national song were played softly on a harp and violin. She tenderly kissed the flag that adorned her and the stage curtain slowly descended. The boisterous crowd demanded another encore and finally she consented to speak to her admirers.

In a very emotional voice she said, "I thank you for this reception, for the beautiful flowers and the flag and music. This Polish flag has more significance than perhaps was intended for I cannot think of my poor, suffering, oppressed country without tears coming to my eyes. You know I am no longer allowed to visit Polish-Russia and cannot visit my friends. I will never again appear before you, but I shall always remember this reception."

When the sentimental actress left the stage everyone in the opera house was truly touched. As Madame Modjeska entered her dressing room, she discovered it had been converted into a fashionable salon with thick carpets covering the floor and festoons of flowers everywhere. It reminded her of the *Poland* car she occupied in 1882 during the Modjeska-Barrymore engagements. Added to the unexpected decor of the dressing room was a bust of Abraham Lincoln prominently displayed in reverence to his birthday. The flower arrangements were later placed in the lobby of the Mission Inn for the public to enjoy.

The day following her farewell appearance, Frank Miller hosted an elegant luncheon in the Mission Inn for the celebrated actress. The large oval table for 15 guests was set with the hotel's finest linen, china and silver. A bowl of fragrant carnations occupied the center of the table. Draped on the ornate buffet was the silk flag that had been presented to her the previous night. Modjeska sat at the head of the table and occupied the large chair made for President Theodore Roosevelt when he visited the Mission Inn in 1903. The Count and Mrs. Bacon sat on either side with friends and hotel guests completing the table. The service was the finest the hotel could produce and the special occasion was deemed a huge success.

That afternoon, the actress left town for her next farewell performance in Salt Lake City. Long after her departure, the story of Frank Miller's presentation of the Polish flag continued to appear in newspaper articles across the country. In Zona Gale's book, *Frank Miller of the Mission Inn*, the story is repeated and she elaborates that Miller attempted to obtain the flag of every visitor "of whose presence he could learn in time." The episode of Modjeska's Polish flag has been repeated so often that it has become a Riverside legend.

In the interval between Madame Modjeska's two Riverside performances in 1899 and 1906, another prominent but controversial public figure passed through the doors of the Mission Inn. Carrie Nation, "Saloon Smasher," came to Riverside in 1903 to promote her cause and soon found that not all guests were greeted with open arms.

Chapter 13

CARRIE AMELIA MOORE NATION
1846-1911

When aging Carrie Nation appeared on the stage of the Loring Opera House on February 19, 1903, faint applause greeted the stout, gray haired "Saloon Smasher." The modest audience of less than 50 had paid 25 cents each to hear her lecture on rum and its evils. Although she was an imposing figure, nearly six feet tall, her high-pitched, overly exuberant voice soon emptied the theater. Newspaper accounts the following day reported that her performance was simply not very entertaining.

In spite of her poor reception in Riverside, a local reporter interviewed the reformer in her third floor suite in the new Glenwood Mission Inn. She was attired in plain, simple clothing and a white silk scarf, adorned only by a small round button depicting a hatchet and inscribed "Defender of Homes." It was the symbol of her cause to rid the world of alcohol. The discreet reporter directed his questions to current affairs rather than her controversial activities and crusades.

Details of her background were common knowledge, including an early tragedy that was to change the course of her life. In 1867, at age 21, Carrie married Dr. Charles Gloyd, a physician, and as it turned out, an alcoholic. This was her first experience with the disease and in spite of her efforts to rehabilitate him he soon died. The young widow then became a staunch opponent of the use of alcohol and an outspoken activist on the subject.

In 1877 she married David Nation, a non-drinking clergyman and attorney. They settled in Kansas where the use of liquor was illegal and the new Mrs. Nation joined the Woman's Christian Temperance Union, an outgrowth of the earlier Woman's Temperance Crusade. Her husband strongly supported and encouraged her membership in this group of Christian women who opposed the sale and use of alcohol. Although the earlier WTC women limited their activities to entering saloons to pray for lost souls, sing religious hymns and denounce the evils of liquor, the Kansas WCTU was undergoing a noticeable transition. The women began invading saloons in a hostile manner for the express purpose of destroying the premises, often foregoing their prayers for lost souls.

With hatchets in hand they aggressively wrecked countless saloons, some where liquor was sold legally, for which they were often arrested and incarcerated for destroying private property. Needless to say, Carrie Nation and friends were unwelcome in most towns.

Mrs. Nation led the well-organized raids to smash every "joint" in town and male guards were used to protect the women from personal injury. The protesters would rendezvous, pray and discuss their plan of action, urging the townspeople, including men, to join their crusade. Usually it was Carrie Nation who provided the leadership necessary to carry out the destruction of saloons scattered throughout Iowa and Kansas. Devoted followers believed she had been called by the Lord to do this work and therefore they would not condemn her actions. Individuals expressed the belief that if the demon liquor should injure one of their loved ones, they too would go after it with hatchet in hand.

On a January afternoon in 1901, Carrie Nation and two women helpers stormed several saloons in Wichita, Kansas. They quickly smashed windows and furniture with their hatchets and completely wrecked the premises. As a result of their actions the three were arrested and jailed for "malicious destruction of property." The owners of the buildings, not the operators of the saloons, filed formal complaints. While the women were incarcerated, 50 men surrounded the jail and picketed in protest of the damage to personal property. An attempt to take Carrie Nation from her cell for a dose of tar and feathers was quickly squelched by the sheriff when he fired his gun in the air.

Members of the Wichita Women's Christian Temperance Union proclaimed Carrie Nation's raid a complete victory and celebrated with a rally at their headquarters. Enthusiastic reaction ran so high that 20 women signed pledges to accompany Mrs. Nation on future raids. Not everyone was pleased with the recent saloon smashing however. The husband of one of the arrested women threatened divorce if she continued her vicious raids. In time even members of the WCTU disapproved of Carrie Nation's methods and withdrew legal and financial support.

The Women's Christian Temperance Union was organized in 1874 with the help of educator and early reformer Frances Willard. She became the first president and leader of the prohibition movement that brought her fame and international recognition. She wrote and lectured about the evils of drink and worked through churches and schools to reach young children. In 1883 Miss Willard visited Riverside as the guest of the local WCTU and addressed a large audience in the Pavilion. She favored the Prohibition Party because it supported a constitutional prohibition amendment and advocated the vote for women. Many comments by Miss Willard were well received as she expressed notable power of thought and conviction. Some pioneer settlers of Riverside, who had originally established the colony as a saloon free community, had long endorsed a strong temperance movement.

When Frances Willard visited Riverside, she was an honored guest in the Glenwood Hotel. The same hospitable reception greeted Susan B. Anthony when she was also a guest at the Glenwood. Townspeople were pleased to hear these dignified ladies who were well educated and spoke sincerely of their compelling causes. Most schools and churches endorsed the early methods of the prohibitionist who prayed, sang hymns and freely distributed their literature. The same public acceptance, however, was not always extended to Carrie Nation who waged war on her own terms against all saloons and their owners.

As a national organization, members of the WCTU wore small white ribbons to identify themselves and their stand against any alcohol. Members of the Riverside chapter paid membership fees of a dollar a year for the privilege of wearing the white ribbons. Many women found the dues expensive but continued to fight the evils of drink. The sale of ribbons was only one means of raising money to carry on the persistent work of the organization that included the publication of educational articles. A large variety of temperance materials were published and distributed to schools and churches to educate children about the dangers of alcohol and the sinful misery it could cause. A devoted member of Riverside's Women's Christian Temperance Union printed much of this literature that was distributed throughout the world.

Stella Irvine became superintendent of the World Sunday School program sponsored by the WCTU. Her impressive house on the southwest corner of First and Brockton became a meeting place for church related groups. She converted part of her 16-room house into workrooms for distribution of Sunday School lessons. A printing press was installed in the basement and massive worktables were scattered throughout the house. International chapters worked together on a variety of different programs all aimed to abolish the sale of alcohol.

In order to finance some of the desired programs of the organization, Carrie Nation consented to a nation-wide lecture tour in 1903. Managers of the tour, however, mistakenly introduced her to California by first booking her in a large Los Angeles theater. As a result, bad publicity and cold receptions followed her performances throughout the state.

Whenever she lectured, she held a thick Bible in her hands from which she quoted page after page in a monotonous tone. She frequently mentioned her personal life and boasted that she had been jailed 13 times, "put there by Republicans you know." She claimed Republicans were the roots of all evil, especially rich ones who were trying to put saloons back in Kansas. "The Democrats want the Republicans out so they can run the saloons. The Democrats would be just as bad in power because big trusts between government and the brewers exist. I am not smashing saloons anymore, but I'm going after the government. I belong to the party of God who established the Prohibition Party. God's laws are all prohibitions." Needless to say, Carrie Nation endorsed the Prohibition Party stating that government officials were in the saloon business since they were benefiting from internal revenue taxes and business licenses. Despite her earlier vindictive attitudes she had stopped smashing saloons by 1903 and began to point her hatchet at "the government that allowed saloons to exist." She claimed she was going to smash the government as hard as she had the saloons.

During her brief stay in Riverside, Mrs. Nation was pleased to be interviewed by the local reporter for she had little company. When asked about her impressions of the town, she reluctantly replied they were very limited. She went on to explain that she was obligated to remain in her room and not appear in public. This was due to a general desire to see her rather than to hear her messages. For that reason she kept to the privacy of her rooms where no one could see her.

Meanwhile, she had some definite opinions about the town that she freely shared with the reporter. She thought Riverside to be a beautiful place with some advantages not all its people appreciated. For one thing, "its money is spent in legitimate business and not on the saloon keeper." No doubt she had been informed there were at least 21 churches and no saloons in town at that time.

During Carrie Nation's visit to the Mission Inn, preparations were under way for the official grand opening of the new Glenwood Mission

Inn to take place on Washington's birthday. Everything in the hotel appeared to be new and spotless for the patriotic flag raising ceremony in the large front courtyard. Mrs. Nation expressed a childish delight in her surroundings and praised the new hotel to be the finest and most home-like place she had ever visited. However, she confided to the reporter her displeasure of a decorative plaque displayed in the lobby. It depicted a group of happy friars prancing around a flowing bowl of wine.She quickly reassured the reporter when she stated, "I don't like it but I shall not smash it."

As the interview ended, the reporter was presented a small hatchet pin as a memento from a domineering woman whose emotions and unfortunate personal experiences led her to violence instead of reasonable actions. He discovered that she was spending her money to build a home in Kansas for wives of alcoholics where they could live in peace. He concluded, "Mrs. Nation is evidently not a crazy woman but one who speaks from her convictions and speaks right to the point."

Chapter 14

FRANCES VAN DE GRIFT STEVENSON
1840 - 1914

In March 1898 Frances Stevenson visited her brother Jake Van de Grift in Riverside and caused considerable curiosity among the residents. As the unconventional widow of the famous writer Robert Louis Stevenson, her Bohemian life-style was public knowledge and well known. The chubby non-conformist wore short hair, loose fitting clothes and rolled her own cigarettes. Nonetheless her only brother was delighted to have Fanny and her family in Riverside. The travelers stayed in the Glenwood Hotel just two blocks from the Van de Grift home on Orange Street.

Jake and his wife Jeannette hosted a grand reception in their home to celebrate Fanny Stevenson's 58th birthday. The party also served as a hearty farewell on the eve of her departure for Europe where she planned to live for two years. Although stormy weather prevailed that evening more than one hundred people came to meet the famous author's wife. Some curiosity seekers came just to observe the adventuresome woman who had lived in the South Seas and had nursed her sick husband until his death. A general invitation appeared in local newspapers and the occasion attracted a variety of people from the community.

The large two-story Van de Grift house was filled with music and animated conversations. Flowers and greenery adorned the rooms and a small ensemble provided soft background music. Fanny Stevenson and her married daughter, Isobel Strong greeted guests who welcomed them to Riverside and conveyed birthday greetings to Fanny. She told her Riverside friends that she, her daughter and her son's family would soon leave for the East Coast via the Southern Pacific on a leisurely trip before departing to Europe. Together they would collaborate on a biography of Robert Louis Stevenson, relying on their intimate knowledge and deep love for him. Before Fanny Stevenson left town she made arrangements for her brother to handle her investments in order to provide a reliable income.

As the widow of Robert Louis Stevenson, Fanny had inherited a sizeable estate from her husband's Scottish parents. In addition she was receiving large royalty checks from his popular books and other publications. During his short lifetime, Robert Louis Balfour Stevenson wrote some of the most enduring stories that continue to attract both young and adult readers. Nearly every English-speaking child knew of his famous book *A Child's Garden of Verse*. His entertaining adventure and romantic fiction books were read worldwide and translated into most foreign languages. Fanny Stevenson relied on her brother Jake who became her financial advisor, trusted real estate partner, and manager of her Riverside properties.

Again in January 1904 Fanny Stevenson came to Riverside with her personal maid and stayed in the new Glenwood Mission Inn. The 64-year-old widow found the hotel accommodations much improved since her last visit adding to her enjoyment. Fanny's visit however was not all leisure. Her brother and partner, Jake Van de Grift, reviewed their real estate investments and inspected several parcels that had been acquired in her absence. She was pleased with the results and knowledge that their holdings were in excess of $40,000.

Her investments included an average looking store on Eighth Street, known as University Avenue today, between Main and Market streets in busy downtown. The property was occupied by the Eighth Street Pool Hall which she later referred to as her dive. She took great pride in telling others that she owned a pool hall and was amused by their shocked reactions.

Another acquisition was located on Main Street adjacent to the Loring Building, a three-story brick structure built in 1890 known as the Fredericks Building. The extensive ground floor was leased to a furniture store with 18 rooms above rented for living quarters. This building was considered her best investment for which she received one hundred dollars per month,

Her other property was a 15-acre citrus grove on the southeast corner of Eighth and Kansas streets. This agricultural land was her pride and joy as it was a reminder of her happy days spent in the South Sea Islands. Years after Fanny Stevenson first saw her grove, the site became the location of University Heights Junior High School, known today as Bobby Bonds Park. Jake managed his sister's properties well and kept her informed of Riverside's real estate market. They maintained a close relationship that dated back to Indianapolis when Fanny, the eldest of six children, adored her only brother.

At the age of 17, Fanny Van de Grift had married Şam Osbournę and thus began an adventuresome life that eventually took her around the world. Her early married life began in remote Nevada mining towns where Sam followed the latest silver strikes, most often without success. Out of necessity Fanny quickly learned to cook, roll her own cigarettes and to handle firearms. Although they had three children, his infidelity and irresponsibility led to a divorce and she took her children to Paris where she studied painting and her youngest child died.

In 1876, she met a young freelance writer, Robert Louis Stevenson, then traveling through Europe. Although he had shaggy long hair and disheveled clothing and suffered from a chronic lung ailment, she was attracted to this fun loving Bohemian. They both subsequently traveled to San Francisco where in 1880 40-year-old Fanny married 29-year old Stevenson. They traveled in Europe for the next seven years seeking a moderate climate to improve his health and when this failed they chartered a yacht and sailed to the South Pacific.

As Stevenson's health improved in the tropical climate, they decided to make the South Seas their permanent home and after several months in the Hawaiian Islands they settled in Samoa. Stevenson purchased three hundred acres of land and built a house called *Vailima*. The family, including Fanny's children, enjoyed a simple, quiet life and grew their own fruits and vegetables. Fanny Stevenson managed the household, nursed her husband and supervised his affairs. It was here that Robert Louis Stevenson wrote many of his books that were read throughout the world. He frequently sought the opinions of his wife and her grown children in the course of his writing.

Life at *Vailima* suited Fanny Stevenson. She chose to wear loose clothes, short hair and to become involved with her garden. Despite her busy life, she kept in close touch with her brother Jake Van de Grift in Riverside and they corresponded regularly. When Fanny read of the unusual Washington navel orange production in Riverside, she asked her brother to send seeds for her garden. In response he wrote back that the navel orange was seedless and thus had to be grafted onto other citrus trees.

In December 1894, Riverside newspapers carried the sad news that Robert Louis Stevenson had died. The next day another news item reported that Stevenson's uncle, Dr. Balfour of Edinburgh, claimed that it was not his nephew who died but probably Fanny. His conclusion was based on his earlier treatment of her for an aneurysm. For three weeks, Jake Van de Grift did not know who had died and finally a message from his sister Fanny confirmed that Robert Louis Stevenson had indeed died.

Fanny Stevenson left her Samoan home and settled in San Francisco where she continued to wear Mother Hubbard clothes and short hair in the comfortable tradition of the tropics. She took pleasure in her avant-garde, Bohemian attire. Ultimately Fanny Stevenson became a wealthy woman and carried a great deal of influence in literary circles. Her brother Jake had invested her money wisely.

The 15-acre citrus grove at Eighth and Kansas was Fanny Stevenson's favorite Riverside property and she enjoyed her role as citrus grower, even though she was an absentee owner. She owned 15 shares of East Riverside Water stock for irrigation purposes and her brother tended to the details. It is not known where her fruit was processed as there were at least 34 packers and shippers in operation in 1904. Poorly constructed packinghouses often went up in flames destroying grower's records.

A year after her visit to the Mission Inn in 1904, Fanny Stevenson once again made the gossip columns. It was reported that she had become involved with a young man 40 years her junior, Edward Field, who lived with her as a "secretary-companion." She maintained residences in San Francisco, Gilroy, Santa Barbara and Mexico, traveling from place to place always accompanied by Field. It was in Santa Barbara on February 14, 1914, that she died at the age of 74 with Edward Field at her side. The cause of death was attributed to a brain hemorrhage, by coincidence the same malady that struck down her late husband, Robert Louis Stevenson.

Before her death Fanny and her brother had divided their jointly owned Riverside investments and her estate was valued at $120,500. The bulk of her estate was left to Isobel, the daughter by her first husband, Sam Osbourne. She inherited the two remaining Riverside properties, the Fredericks Building and the 15-acre citrus grove, the pool hall having been previously sold. Fanny's will also provided for her son Lloyd Osbourne, who was to receive $300 per month for the remainder of his life. He had been financially dependent on his mother and had lived in her San Francisco house for years.

Isobel's first marriage had ended in divorce many years earlier when her mother and stepfather were living in Samoa. After Fanny's death, she married Edward Field, her mother's former companion. Some years later her husband Edward Field and her brother Lloyd Osbourne became playwrights and Broadway producers.

Frances Van de Grift Osbourne Stevenson was an eccentric woman who deviated from the generally accepted standards of society and relished every opportunity to display her independence. Whenever she passed through the doors of the Mission Inn she drew stares from guests and employees alike who may have disapproved but always remembered the strange lady with the distinctive clothing and short hair.

Another hotel guest who also wore non-conforming attire was Elbert Hubbard who became a good friend of Frank Miller in spite of their different lifestyles.

Chapter 15

ELBERT HUBBARD
1856-1915

When Frank Miller first met Elbert Hubbard during the summer of 1902, it was the beginning of a long, close relationship that spanned the continent from East Aurora, New York to Riverside, California. That summer Miller and his wife Isabella were traveling to inspect several eastern hotels while their new Glenwood Mission Inn was under construction. They visited Albert and Alfred Smiley's renowned resort at Lake Mohonk, Paul Smith's popular hotel in the Adirondacks and Elbert Hubbard's Roycroft Inn. It was Hubbard, however, who impressed the Millers with his magnetic personality and innovative advertising and marketing skills. They developed a lifelong friendship.

Ten years before the Frank Millers visited New York, Elbert Hubbard had retired as a successful salesman with the Larkin Soap Manufacturing Company in Buffalo. He had implemented lucrative promotional sales tactics such as extending credit to known customers, offering premium prizes for large orders and he introduced mail order sales to new markets. By the age of 36 Hubbard had accumulated sufficient funds to pursue his desire to write and travel in Europe. While visiting England he became intrigued with the talents and philosophy of William Morris, poet, artist and designer of furniture. The distinguished Englishman headed a company that manufactured useful household items and practical pieces of furniture, including the popular Morris chair. In addition, the talented Morris engaged in the art of decorative printing with intricate border designs. Elbert Hubbard was truly inspired by the remarkable talents of William Morris, a man he admired and revered.

When Hubbard returned home in 1894, he became an advocate of the Arts and Crafts Movement featuring simple designed furniture for everyday use. The following year he founded the Roycroft Shop named for seventeenth century English printers Thomas and Samuel Roycroft. In East Aurora he opened a print shop and published a periodical entitled *The Philistine*. It featured stories setting forth his personal views on a number of subjects ranging from political influences to defining the fine points of playing baseball. Because of his uninhibited writing on diverse topics, he soon gained a cult-like following of devoted readers. In addition the Roycroft Press produced beautifully bound books in the tradition of medieval craftsmen which were often numbered and signed by Hubbard. Other elaborate publications included journals and magazines with full-page advertisements for Roycroft furniture.

Soon after opening the inspiring Roycroft Shop, Elbert Hubbard issued a public invitation to any and all artisans who wished to pursue their creative craft skills and encouraged them to join his utopian community in East Aurora. The response to this invitation was overwhelming and completely unexpected. An army of artistic craftsmen gathered and with Hubbard's guidance the diverse crowd established the Roycroft Colony. The mixture of people became a self-contained village with their own bank, post office, baseball team and marching band. Free medical services, clothing, educational and recreational facilities were all provided with income generated from the sales of handcrafted articles sold in the Roycroft Shop. It was a congenial entity where aesthetics and commerce were combined into a flourishing community.

To accommodate the increasing number of tourists visiting East Aurora, Hubbard built a rustic English Tudor style hotel named the Roycroft Inn. The carpentry shop manufactured Arts and Crafts style furniture to fill the hotel rooms. The simple furniture reflected fine craftsmanship of the resident artisans and hotel guests were soon inquiring where they might purchase such beautifully finished pieces. Elbert Hubbard came up with several brilliant ideas. He circulated a mail order catalog picturing available furniture and easy steps to order Roycroft articles. To provide a wider market, the entrepreneur opened outlet stores in several major cities in the east. Furthermore, every piece of furniture in the rooms of the Roycroft Inn had a discreet price tag attached whereby guests could purchase items and charge them to their room. To eliminate sales of copies, Hubbard had the Roycroft emblem placed on each piece of furniture signifying its authenticity. An emblem with a double armed cross with a circle enclosing the letter R at its base was impressed or embossed on Roycroft items. Individual specialty shops were established in the Roycroft community for the convenience of guests who wandered from store to store. The Press and Bindery Shop produced superior books dealing with literature and art. The Copper Shop made wrought iron objects such as lamps and andirons. Leftover pieces of leather from the bookbinding department furnished material to make bookmarks stamped with the Roycroft emblem. In order to sell more Roycroft artifacts, Elbert Hubbard established a lecture tour and traveled around the United States annually. As the ultimate salesman, he easily sold himself to conventional crowds who often came to "see and hear the Bohemian dandy." Due to his personal appearances he increased the Roycroft sales and gained hundreds of subscriptions for his various publications. With his picturesque and commanding personality, he entertained audiences throughout the country with his frank off-the-cuff remarks.

In February 1905, the eccentric New Yorker and his second wife Alice visited the Mission Inn. He had established himself as an outrageous character with a mop of shaggy hair and a rumpled cowboy appearance. As a non-conformist, he wore wide brimmed cowboy hats and soft scarf ties. Needless to say whenever he appeared at public gatherings, this distinct character was readily noticed. Elbert Hubbard thrived on the spontaneous attention he created and enjoyed being known as a true American personality. His arrival at the Mission Inn was fittingly recorded in the *Riverside Daily Press*.

Elbert Hubbard was impressed with Frank Miller's Mission Inn because it typified early California's warm hospitality and quiet setting. He felt quite at home with the hotel's furnishing of sturdy simple chairs with tooled leather seats and other furnishings that resembled Roycroft items. Frank Miller purchased several pieces of Arts and Crafts style furniture from the Roycroft Shops and Gustav Stickley. When Elbert Hubbard returned to New York, he wrote complimentary articles about Riverside's fantastic Mission Inn and its ingenious creators, Frank and Isabella Miller. The friendship between Hubbard and Miller was a most unlikely liaison since their life styles were so diverse. Frank Miller, a strict Congregationalist, led a Puritan life while Hubbard was considered an activist.

In 1908, Hubbard started a new publication called *The Fra*. It was a journal containing articles with fewer personal opinions and more of the public's accepted views. Hubbard, who began identifying himself as "Fra Elbertus" and adopted the title Fra – a reference to a monk or religious brother.

Hubbard, his wife and daughter Miriam, toured southern California in the spring of 1909 and spent two days visiting his good friend Frank Miller at the Mission Inn. He missed Isabella Miller who had died the year before and he publicly announced "she was one of the really great women of the century." He addressed Miller as "Fra Frank" on many occasions and then dubbed him "Masterful Frank." Ever the promoter, Hubbard carried the pretentious name dropping a step further and referred to Frank Miller as "Master of the Inn." This title is still in use today when referring to Frank Miller and his grand hotel.

Frank Miller entertained the Hubbards with a personally conducted tour of the city including a leisurely drive over the wooden Victoria Bridge spanning the Tequesquite Arroyo. The party continued down scenic Victoria Avenue and turned onto Magnolia Avenue near the Sherman Institute. This 40-acre Indian boarding school was a federal facility where some 500 students lived and attended school. In addition, the boys and girls were offered a variety of vocational subjects including carpentry, a class that intrigued Elbert Hubbard. The students were working on furniture utilizing the Arts and Crafts designs of Stickley and Roycroft. Hubbard highly praised the boys and encouraged them to continue producing quality-handcrafted furniture and cabinets.

The highlight of their Riverside tour, however, was a ride on the narrow, dirt road to the top of Mount Rubidoux that had been constructed since Hubbard's last visit. The tourists were thrilled to observe the panoramic view of the entire valley from atop the mountain. Hubbard filled the Loring Theater that evening with an attentive audience even though he had been labeled Frank Miller's "ungodly friend." Because of his unconventional approach to politics and literature, he was often regarded with suspicion and skepticism. Nevertheless, the Loring Theater audience listened intently when told of the 500 people living and working in his Roycroft establishment. He announced that he might add another Roycroft Shop in California and many speculated it could be located in Riverside's Mission Inn. The shop did not materialize, however, as he became more engrossed in writing and publishing and less in Roycroft business.

After returning to East Aurora, Hubbard produced several artistic booklets describing the charms to be found at the Mission Inn. One was entitled *Days of Peace and Rest at the Glenwood by Those Who Know* and this was followed by *Music at Meal Times*. He even implied that the hotel site had once been occupied by a California mission, a fact he knew to be untrue.

In May 1915, he and his wife sailed for England despite the beginning of World War I. He wrote to a friend in Milwaukee before departing on the Cunard liner, *Lusitania.* stating, "If I get back, if I do, perhaps I'll meet with a mine or a submarine." There had been definite warnings that the Germans might attack the giant liner because they believed it was carrying war material. The world was nevertheless shocked when the liner was hit by a German torpedo and sank within 15 minutes. More than 1300 passengers were lost at sea including the flamboyant Elbert Hubbard and his wife.

Frank Miller adopted several of Elbert Hubbard's brilliant business practices. He established a carpentry shop in the hotel and hired skilled craftsmen to manufacture and repair furniture. He designated the Indian Rain Cross as the Mission Inn logo and displayed it throughout the hotel. After the 1910 Cloister Wing was added, Miller installed an extensive curio shop for the convenience of his guests and the general public. Price tags were discreetly attached to most items in the hotel and guests could charge a purchase to their room. Elbert Hubbard was a clever, flamboyant businessman who had the knack of knowing that the American public would pay for comfortable surroundings and quality merchandise.

Chapter 16

NAPOLEON AND FRIENDS
1907-1956

Two brightly colored Brazilian macaws were once familiar sights perched near the entrance of the Mission Inn. They were named Napoleon and Joseph, not Josephine as might be expected. For many years these beautiful long tailed birds greeted the famous and not so famous people who passed through the doors of the Mission Inn.

In the 1890s Joseph was a gift to the Miller family from a San Diego sailor who had recently returned from South America and the bird was assumed to be a year old. Joseph's bright red feathers extended from the top of his beak to the tip of his long, pointed tail. His brilliant blue wings were outlined in yellow and gold feathers and the combination of colors made Joseph a magnificent sight. He was the patriarch of the Mission Inn menagerie.

When the 1903 Mission Inn opened, Joseph and other pet birds moved into the new building. Polly, a dignified green parrot came to the Glenwood Hotel in the 1890s, a gift of local socialite Grace Gilliland. Polly was a talker and continually uttered "Polly wants a cracker." She would beg for peanuts and seeds and hold out her foot for treats and then snuggle up to her benefactor as a thank you gesture. Joseph and Polly were close companions and spent their days together in the trees in the front courtyard.

Another bird that moved from the Glenwood Hotel into the new building was an unnamed male green parrot from the Philippine Islands. He perched daily on tree branches extending over the corner of Orange and Seventh streets and uttered loud salutes to passing pedestrians. He attracted attention from unsuspecting walkers, downtown merchants and businessmen who often returned his calls.

In 1896, Opal, a white Australian cockatoo, became a Mission Inn resident. What she lacked in brilliant plumage she made up in friendly exuberance. Her constant companion was a large green and yellow Mexican parrot named Patrick. Whenever she was not present, Patrick kept up a constant irritating squawk until her return. One morning in 1915 after Opal had spent the night in her indoor cage, she made a terrible fuss. A bellman finally came to calm her down and discovered a lone egg in the bottom of her cage. Twenty year-old Opal wanted the world to know she had produced her first and only egg. Many years later in 1936, the famous aviatrix Amelia Earhart visited the Inn and had her picture taken with Opal on her shoulder.

It was not unusual for resort hotels to maintain pets and small zoos to entertain and amuse their guests. When the popular Hotel Del Coronado closed in 1902 for extensive remodeling, its small collection of animals was given to the Riverside Chemawa Park Zoo. Frank Miller managed the 30-acre park, owned and operated by a local streetcar company. Animals from the Del Coronado were transported to Riverside in custom made crates designed to accommodate six monkeys, three deer, an alligator, three parrots and two macaws. The animals arrived safely and were housed in enclosed pens in the amusement park on Magnolia Avenue.

In 1903, the same year Joseph, Polly and Opal settled into the Glenwood Mission Inn, Frank Miller ordered 14 tree squirrels. They were released to run freely around the front courtyard known as the Court of the Birds. The squirrels learned to beg for peanuts and hotel guests gladly obliged. Jerry became the favorite because he wasn't shy and when he died in 1908, newspapers reported that he was the best known squirrel in the world.

One day in 1906, before Napoleon's arrival, Joseph disappeared and the Millers sent out a desperate plea for his safe return. The red feathered bird had complete freedom and was allowed to fly within or without the hotel grounds. When he hadn't returned to his usual perch on the third floor balcony after dark, Isabella Miller became concerned about Joseph, her favorite pet. Later that night, the wayward bird returned to the relief of his many admirers. Several days later, the Millers had his wings clipped effectively ending his flying episodes. Other Mission Inn pet birds subsequently suffered the same fate requiring long poles to lift them into high branches. After Joseph could no longer fly he encountered a frisky puppy and the defenseless bird lost all but one of his magnificent tail feathers, a sorry sight.

Napoleon, a native of Brazil, arrived at the Mission Inn in 1907 as a gift for Frank Miller from an anonymous friend. Soon after his arrival, he was regarded as the monarch of all bird residents. His appearance resembled one of Napoleon's uniformed soldiers with bright blue plumage covering most of his body. His chest had yellow feathers with a patch of black in the center. Napoleon's most unusual feature was the narrow black lines encircling his eyes that appeared to have been painted. Whenever hotel guests discussed this possibility, Mission Inn personnel informed them it was not possible because Napoleon was a cranky, bad tempered bird not easily curtailed.

After Napoleon arrived, there was a change in the bird dynasty, as he became the dominant member of the family. He proudly rode on the shoulder of his master, Frank Miller, and roamed through the courtyard and lobby to greet guests. Each morning Napoleon and Joseph were brought from their overnight quarters inside the hotel and placed on perches near the front entrance. Although neither bird could actually talk, these brightly colored creatures attracted considerable attention. They thrived in the fresh air, sunshine, and fruit and nuts offered by visitors. Conscientious employees, such as Billy Herbert and John Allen, supervised the care of Napoleon and Joseph and gave them their daily quota of cashew nuts and seeds. On special occasions, the birds were allowed to bath and play in the lawn sprinklers to the amusement of the guests.

When members of the Audubon Society met in the Mission Inn in 1909, Frank Miller welcomed the crowd and thanked state legislators who had passed the Audubon Bill assuring the protection of songbirds. He stated, "California's feathered songsters are always welcome at the Mission Inn. Their presence is deemed an honor by the management and the birds are fed and made to feel at home. The songs of the birds and their presence in the trees of the courtyard is an added charm that we encourage and welcome." Pigeons and other birds found safe havens for their nests in the many recessed nooks and eves in the Mission Inn. For a time owls were regular residents who kept the stray rodents under control.

The Mission Inn bird population noticeably increased in the 1940s whenever Mrs. Ulysses Grant McQueen of Beverly Hills was in residence. Founder of the Women's International Association of Aeronautics, Elizabeth McQueen was a good friend of Frank Miller's daughter, Allis Hutchings. She was an interesting character who lived at the Inn for extended periods of time. She always brought her pet birds and they received the same attention as Napoleon and Joseph. Dick, her pet parrot, could skillfully whistle tunes from grand opera and charmed the ladies with his sweet words of endearment. Another green parrot named Guate spoke Spanish only and few people knew for sure what he was saying.

Perhaps the most unusual and unwelcome critter to make itself comfortable in the Mission Inn appeared mysteriously one morning in 1951. A gardener working near the rock fountain in the Court of the Birds, noticed two shiny eyes staring from within some shrubbery. Thinking it was an alley cat, he tried to shoo it away with his rake but no matter how much he prodded the "cat" wouldn't budge. Finally he told management of the unknown animal lurking in the bushes and the dog-catcher was summoned. After several unsuccessful attempts the police were called and they too poked at the bushes for some time without success. As a last resort, the officer shot the lurking animal that turned out to be a four-foot long bobcat. Where it came from and how it got into the Court of the Birds remained a mystery. Sometime later, however, it was discovered that two exotic fish planted in the pond at the foot of the waterfall were missing. No doubt, the wayward bobcat had eaten a gourmet last supper.

On another occasion shortly thereafter, a gray fox found its way to the top floor of the International Rotunda where it was cornered and restrained by Avery Edwin Field. Field operated a photography studio in the building and was no doubt called upon because he was available. Just where the fox came from remained a mystery but since there was some evidence that it had worn a collar, it was concluded that it may have been a pet. The Humane Society rescued the fox but no one claimed it.

During the 1950s, Napoleon gradually began to lose his sight. He eventually went blind in one eye and was losing sight in the other. During cool weather he was kept indoors and pampered by a number of bellmen who cared for him. He had coffee and toast for breakfast and relished his daily allotment of nuts and seeds. One morning in July 1956, he was carried to his favorite roosting spot near the waterfall in the Court of the Birds where he spent most of his declining days removed from the public. Later that day, a gardener found him dead from an apparent heart attack.

Headlines in local papers announced "Napoleon Rules No More" noting that he had been king in the Court of the Birds since 1907. His friends and companions were no longer living and the only remaining bird in the Mission Inn was a parrot named Buddy. Buddy, a green and yellow headed parrot, came to live at the Mission Inn in 1941 after Polly died.

Napoleon was buried on the slopes of Mount Rubidoux, rather than with his old friends and companions who had been laid to rest in the Court of the Birds. Some believed the bird's death reflected a symbolic change in the Mission Inn as within weeks, the Fairmont Hotel Corporation purchased the Mission Inn after 80 years of Miller ownership.

Napoleon had outlived members of the Miller family who protected and cared for him all his life. He had been Frank Miller's favorite macaw and thus enjoyed special privileges and treats. During Napoleon's long life, he had greeted President William Howard Taft, Henry Ford and Albert Einstein all of whom remembered the appropriately named bird with the blue coat of feathers.

Joseph, the patriarch, and Napoleon, the monarch, have been immortalized throughout the Mission Inn and their colorful images may be found on stained glass windows, ceramic tiles and decorative paintings.

Chapter 17

CHARLES WARREN FAIRBANKS
1852-1918

Charles Fairbanks, vice-president of the United States, spent his last two days in office in Riverside's Mission Inn. His four-year term, under President Theodore Roosevelt, ended in March 1909. Inauguration of the 27th president, William Howard Taft and of vice-president James Sherman took place while Fairbanks and his wife Cornelia were visiting their son Fred in Colton. It was an ideal place to avoid government functions with the changing of the guard. Charles Fairbanks had been a guest in the Inn before and remembered Frank Miller's hospitality.

In 1898 Senator Fairbanks of Indiana was a guest in the Mission Inn and befriended Frank Miller. When he returned to Riverside in 1909 he was duly impressed with the changes that had taken place. He was amazed at the growth and prosperity of the region with its expanded citrus industry and thriving businesses. The six-year old Mission Inn was filled with eastern tourists spending the winter in southern California. When interviewed by local newsmen, he emphasized that his itinerary did not include any politics and he and his family planned to travel extensively. He hoped to visit southern California more frequently, especially the exhilarating Mission Inn.

Charles Fairbanks grew up in Indianapolis and in 1874 passed the Indiana bar examination and started practicing law. He married Cornelia Cole who supported his political endeavors and encouraged him to participate in governmental affairs. Although the couple had six children, Cornelia belonged to various women's organizations as a helpful means to boost her husband's career. When Congress was in session, the Fairbanks maintained a large house on Massachusetts Avenue in Washington, D.C. Charles Fairbanks gained a prestigious reputation as an expert corporate attorney and a specialist in railroad litigation. With this diverse legal background, he became one of the best-known lawyers and financiers in the Midwest.

As a Republican candidate, he was elected to the United States Senate in 1896 and conscientiously served until March 3, 1905. Charles Fairbanks might have been president of the United States had he accepted an invitation in 1900 to run as vice-president on the Republican ticket with William McKinley. McKinley favored Fairbanks but the Senator withdrew from consideration believing he could be of more help remaining in the Senate. The imposing gentlemen were good friends with similar beliefs and political views. Fairbanks reasoned his seat in the Senate, with a vote and the ability to gain other votes, could help influence and support the President's views and decisions. He thought the vice-president's position might be an uninteresting four-year term with a slim chance of renomination.

Theodore Roosevelt, Governor of New York, also declined to run as vice-president; however delegates at the Republican convention in 1900 campaigned and put his name on the ticket. The colorful character was a sentimental choice, a hero in the Spanish-American War and the famed leader of the courageous Rough Riders. Furthermore, a bold, defiant political machine in the state of New York wished to oust Roosevelt in order to stop him from interfering with their dubious business schemes. He accepted the nomination after being informed that to decline would lead to the end of his political career. Another influencing factor in accepting the nomination involved the theory that the office of vice-president could possibly be a stepping stone to the 1904 presidency.

The 1900 Republican convention was a dull affair as most of the candidates had been determined in advance. Senator Fairbanks, a delegate at large, read the Republican platform to the bored crowd. McKinley and Roosevelt were the chosen candidates and delegates returned home and successfully campaigned. They won the national election with little effort and on March 4, 1901, they took office. Six months later, anarchist Leon Czolgosz shot William McKinley in the stomach.

Charles Fairbanks rushed to McKinley's bedside in Buffalo, New York, where the President lingered for days. Their friendship spanned many years and McKinley often sought Fairbank's advice. The two men looked alike, always dignified and proper in similar Prince Albert coats. When it appeared the President was improving his friends left Buffalo and Fairbanks went to a scheduled Grand Army of the Republic (GAR) encampment in Cleveland. When news reached Fairbanks the President was dying, he quickly returned to say farewell and pray for him. McKinley died on September 16, 1901. His assassin pleaded guilty and was put to death after a short trial. Theodore Roosevelt became President of the United States.

Fairbanks extensive knowledge of law and expertise in diplomacy made him a valuable international diplomat. McKinley had appointed him to the Joint-High Commission to determine the United States and Canadian boundary in Alaska. Although there were no immediate decisions, Fairbanks increased his popularity when he stated, "I am opposed to the yielding of an inch of United States Territory." The people of Alaska considered him a hero and to show their appreciation, they named the city of Fairbanks in his honor. This remote, mining camp in the interior of the territory gained its name in 1902 and incorporated in 1903. Later the area was connected by railroads and Fairbanks became known as "The Golden Heart of Alaska."

Delegates to the 1904 Republican convention in Chicago selected Theodore Roosevelt as their presidential candidate after he completed McKinley's term of office. Charles Fairbanks was chosen to run for vice-president. He believed his service would be advantageous to the country and a possible step towards the future presidency. In some circles the second office is regarded as a term of preliminary service before obtaining the higher office. Roosevelt and Fairbanks won the national election and took their respective offices in March 1905.

During their terms of service, Roosevelt's overpowering personality and love of drama made the calm, dignified Fairbanks appear dull and uninteresting. Roosevelt had little enthusiasm for his vice-president and gave him little opportunity to express or use his knowledge of litigation and corporate law. Fairbanks fulfilled his term of office but was regarded as a mere figurehead under the domineering and controlling force of Roosevelt. When Charles Fairbanks had only a few days left in office, he headed for southern California for a change, both climactic and political.

The six-foot-tall, distinguished gentleman came to Riverside to visit his son Fred a citrus grower who lived near the famous Victoria Ranch east of town. At one time the grove was owned by a group of investors that included Charles Fairbanks. Eventually, the property became family owned. The Fairbanks Company packed its fruit under their own label known as the Ostrich Brand. In the center of the label was a giant ostrich and near its feet two babies coming out of their shells. A background of snow-capped mountains, rolling hills covered in citrus tress, tall cactus plants and a mother ostrich was an easily remembered citrus label. After a visit with their son and their stay at the Mission Inn, the Fairbanks returned home to Indiana where he began life as a country gentleman.

In 1911, due to a special invitation from Frank Miller, Charles Fairbanks returned to the Mission Inn. Miller had asked him to be the keynote speaker at the first Peace Conference on the Pacific Coast. The informative conference, primarily financed and advocated by Andrew Carnegie, was held in the new Music Room of the Mission Inn. Many prominent citizens attended the various lectures and discussion groups. Influential men such as naturalist John Muir and author John Burroughs heard Charles Fairbanks describe the peaceful atmosphere found at the Mission Inn and the city of Riverside. "Peace," he claimed "comes from moral impulses and civic pride and together they help the progress of arbitration between nations." The virtues of world peace and how to obtain harmony among all nations brought forth numerous theories and heated discussions. That February, Riverside and the Mission Inn made national news with the presence of so many famous dignitaries seeking world peace.

Charles Fairbanks spent the winter of 1913 in Pasadena and remained out of national politics. Since the death of his wife, he had been in poor health and hoped a winter in southern California might prove beneficial. In January 1914 he visited the Mission Inn and returned again in March for a longer duration. That March the Inn filled to capacity and most of the rooms were occupied the entire month. A new kitchen had been installed and Frank Miller commented, "With modern facilities the hotel could provide meals for a thousand people." The enlarged dining room could accommodate more diners and when the central courtyard patio was completed additional guests could be served.

While 62-year-old Fairbanks was in residence, 25 members of the Chicago White Sox were also staying at the Inn. The baseball team was in Riverside to play an exhibition game with the Los Angeles Angels. Sports fan Fairbanks witnessed the downtown parade on Main Street and waved to ball players riding in convertibles. The crowd followed the cars to Fourteenth Street and entered Evans Park near Brockton. Bleachers filled with enthusiastic fans and Charles Fairbanks made himself comfortable in the packed grandstand. The Sherman Indian Band provided marching music and set the stage for an exciting game. Mayor Oscar Ford threw the first ball to start the game and everyone yelled and whistled. From start to finish spectators vocalized after every play and screamed with every score. After an afternoon watching a slugfest the Chicago White Sox beat the Los Angeles Angels 12 to 8.

A few days later, Charles Fairbanks returned to Pasadena after bidding farewell to his many Riverside friends. In 1916, he ran as a vice-presidential candidate on the Republican ticket with Charles E. Hughes. Woodrow Wilson won the election and became the 28th president of the United States. Ironically, he was deeply devoted to world peace, as was Charles Fairbanks. With this defeat Fairbanks gave up politics and returned to his Indianapolis home and practiced law until his death in 1918. He died at his home from a chronic ailment, surrounded by family members.

Chapter 18

FRANCES TRACY MORGAN
1842-1924

When Mrs. J. P. Morgan, wife of the world's foremost financier, arrived at Riverside's Mission Inn on April 5, 1910, local newspaper reporters were on hand and gave her visit extensive coverage. The name John Pierpont Morgan was synonymous with immense wealth, political influence and world power. The millionaire was a risk taker who controlled entire industries through his shrewd investments and acquisitions of promising companies. His dominance and magnetism extended beyond his business dealings and eventually had an adverse effect on his family life.

John Pierpont Morgan married Frances Louisa Tracy one month after the Civil War ended. Her father, Charles S. Tracy, practiced law in Utica, New York, where he provided a happy, religious home life for his six daughters. On their honeymoon, J. P. took Frances, better known as Fanny, to his parent's home in London. His mother, Juliet Pierpont was the daughter of Reverend John Pierpont, a distinguished Bostonian preacher, poet and patriot. Junius Spencer Morgan, his father, was a partner in a private London bank and was considered the most important financier in England.

Fanny Morgan was a bright, well-educated woman with a shapely figure and pleasing personality. She played tennis with enthusiasm and was an expert equestrian. In the 1870s, the J. P .Morgans lived in a modest house just off Fifth Avenue where Fanny took care of the house and raised four children – Louisa, Juliet, Annie and John Jr. In later years she had a staff of servants who catered to the family's every need.

Although basically shy and often in poor health, Fanny Morgan entertained her husband's influential friends whenever necessary. His business acquaintances were ambitious young entrepreneurs and politicians who had emerged after the Civil War. The country was undergoing a spectacular industrial revolution with the establishment of new industries and companies. Morgan, the astute businessman, became a partner in the banking firm of Drexel, Morgan & Company and it eventually evolved into the J.P. Morgan Company, the largest private financial institution in the world.

When Fanny Morgan's husband became a successful banker they purchased a brownstone mansion on Madison Avenue. The house was unpretentious compared to those of other wealthy New York businessmen. The Morgan home was different in many ways because of his J. P.'s art collections. Displayed throughout the house were exquisite oil paintings and rare books. He had begun collecting European art before his marriage and always considered himself a collector rather than a connoisseur.

The family attended St. George's Episcopal Church and often extended invitations to members for Sunday evening musicals. Mr. Morgan enjoyed singing and looked forward to these gatherings. No one dared to mention that he couldn't carry a tune. In spite of his off-key singing, everyone including Fanny enjoyed these songfests.

The Morgans eventually acquired a country retreat along the Hudson River called *Cragston*. It was an ideal place for the family to escape New York's summer heat and provided a healthy environment for the children. Fanny was in residence from April until early fall and entertained her Tracy family relatives and many friends. The main house contained six bedrooms with several small cottages scattered throughout the property for the staff. Fanny raised prized collies and enjoyed supervising the dog kennels and the awards her pets won. She took a keen interest in the community near *Cragston* and promoted efforts to landscape the area with trees and flowers. Although Fanny was content to stay at the country estate, her husband visited *Cragston* infrequently.

J. P. was an inveterate traveler and in 1869 he was joined by his wife and family members aboard the new transcontinental railroad to California. They long remembered their visit to beautiful Yosemite Valley. Seven years later in 1876, while many people of wealth attended the Philadelphia Centennial Exposition, the Morgan family traveled to Egypt. Nurses and nannies cared for the children as they sailed the Nile River. This was J. P. Morgan's favorite country and he was fascinated with its relics of an earlier civilization. As the wife of an important American capitalist, Fanny's traveling wardrobe consisted of specially designed gowns and hats. Whenever the Morgans traveled throughout the world, Fanny longed to return to her New York brownstone and her country home, *Cragston*.

While Fanny Morgan was less inclined to travel and preferred home life, her vivacious husband continued to travel the world, often in the company of beautiful women. The robust financier was six feet tall, with forceful eyes, a large mustache and an overabundance of energy who thrived in large, boisterous crowds. Socialites and actresses were lavishly entertained aboard his luxurious yachts and plush railroad cars. In 1898, to satisfy his insatiable desire to travel, he replaced his 204-foot yacht, *Corsair II,* with a more modern steam-powered model, the 304-foot *Corsair III.* The new boat expanded his travels to Europe where he held lavish parties for his lady friends and continued to collect works of art for his extensive collections. His trips prompted the rumor that "in addition to old masters, Morgan collects old mistresses." Because of his enormous wealth and political influence, however, his scandalous activities were little noted and in spite of his wanderings, J. P. remained attentive to his children and affectionate to Fanny.

By 1900, Morgan's collections and other possessions had outgrown their New York home and he purchased adjoining property on which to build his private library. He retained the services of the finest craftsmen available for the elaborate Italian Renaissance style building at a cost of over one million dollars. Several years later, he purchased adjacent property as a home site for his daughter Louisa and her husband Herbert Satterlee. The Pierpont Morgan Library located at 29 East 36 Street remains one of New York City's many treasures, a museum filled with rare objects collected by J. P. Morgan and his wife, Fanny.

J. P. was a banker's banker who used funds primarily for investments. In 1905, he acquired perhaps the most valuable piece of property in New York City, the prestigious number One Wall Street. He built a four story financial center of simple design with secure basement vaults and a roof top garden. One morning while en route to the bank police chased his carriage through downtown traffic after they had witnessed his coach strike a lady pedestrian. When ordered to stop the coachman whipped his horse and raced through the financial district. Several mounted police finally caught up with J. P. Morgan's carriage and arrested the driver. During the commotion they noticed a most attractive woman in the cab with the famous banker. Shortly after this incident Morgan was linked with the popular English stage star Maxine Elliott and reportedly financed her New York theater engagement.

The flamboyant banker, known as the financial dictator of the United States, often assisted the government through times of depression. He had a great deal of influence over the nation's economy and was instrumental in corporate expansions and mergers. Morgan created industrial empires in railroads, steel mills, and commercial banks. While men of wealth had double standards of conduct, Victorian Fanny Morgan had no desire to compete with her husband's women. She led her own domestic life surrounded by her children and traveled when and where she pleased.

In February 1908, Fanny Morgan went to California with two of her lady friends. They traveled in the luxurious car, *Independence,* rumored to cost $50,000. Upon their arrival in Riverside they were driven to the Mission Inn where she informed Frank Miller she wanted a quiet rest and did not wish to be entertained. She was modesty dressed and attracted little attention. Mrs. Morgan was eager to see everything of interest and the ladies were driven around Riverside. When she departed Fanny expressed a desire to have a winter home in the "city of golden oranges."

Two years later in the spring of 1910 after J. P. Morgan left for Europe, Fanny returned to California. She wanted a change of scenery and believed the warmer climate might improve her health. She invited four of her lady friends to accompany her in the Morgan's Palace car named *Magnate.* After a leisurely trip they arrived in Riverside and again she told Frank Miller that she wanted a quiet rest. This may have been welcome news to Miller who was then preparing the hotel for an elite group of eastern hotel executives who would require his full attention.

By 1910, the Mission Inn was nationally known and well patronized by American tourists. There were 300 guestrooms, each slightly different from the other. The expansive dining room prompted a quiet, refined atmosphere and demure waitresses could be gently summoned by small bell signals. Starched, white table clothes and blue glazed china covered the tables and guests could chose a chair with or without arms. The recently completed Cloister Wing, or monastery, contained additional space for large banquets and a most intriguing underground corridor referred to as the Catacombs. In each hotel room, guests were presented a *Book of Welcome.* Enclosed in a decorative envelope were a number of lovely pictures of the Mission Inn and scenes of flourishing Riverside citrus groves.

During her 1910 stay at the Mission Inn, Fanny and her guests were given the prestigious Presidential Suite, also known as the Roosevelt Suite in recognition of President Theodore Roosevelt's 1903 visit. Upon her arrival, Fanny had requested anonymity and was assured that the suite was well suited for her needs. Not unlike the president, she is believed to have had her own bodyguard inconspicuously lurking not far from her door.

After spending a restful night, Fanny Morgan and her friends awakened to the enchanting chimes of the Mission Inn carillon. The ladies gathered in the lobby to be transported to the *Magnate,* J. P. Morgan's private rail car. While waiting, they had the opportunity to view the beautiful carved wood plaques along the lobby walls depicting classic proverbs and slogans. One such saying in particular symbolized the visit of Mrs. John Pierpont Morgan and is sure to have been remembered: "Next To Love Quietness."

Another hotel guest named Harold Bell Wright could relate to the simple words of wisdom because he also desired privacy and solitude while staying in the Mission Inn.

Chapter 19

HAROLD BELL WRIGHT
1872-1944

In November 1928, Japan's Emperor Hirohito, upon his accession to the throne, honored Frank Miller for his accomplishments in promoting world peace and goodwill among nations. The Emperor's representatives bestowed on Miller the coveted Order of the Rising Sun at stately ceremonies held in the Mission Inn. Accounts of the presentation were reported nationwide and reached Harold Bell Wright, who responded with a congratulatory note to his close friend, Alice Miller Richardson: "Good for the Japanese government. It is grand to know that some people are yet able to recognize men in this world and age. Please convey to your brother Frank my hearty congratulations and say that the Japanese have nothing on me for I decorated him years ago in my heart."

Although Wright was 15 years younger than Miller, they were good friends who shared many common beliefs and sentiments. Both were products of modest Christian families and devoted to their church. They believed that the essential qualities of a first-class citizen consisted of courage, honesty, usefulness and sincerity. In addition both were supporters of the great southwest and the preservation of its historic artifacts and natural beauty.

One of four boys, Wright was raised in New York where his mother died at an early age and his father worked as a carpenter. His interest in America's southwest was acquired in his later years from his travels as a writer, painter and minister. When Harold was 20 he had saved enough money to enroll in the Preparatory Department of Hiram College located near Cleveland, Ohio. Founded by the Disciples of Christ, also known as the Christian Church of Christ, it was a small, co-ed liberal arts school. Members followed the teachings of Christianity as practiced by the Apostles and were sometimes called Campbellites. Hiram College students lived in dormitories and most worked to pay their way through school. Harold painted houses and occasionally engaged in interior decorating. His creative talents led to sketching and painting landscapes that subsequently paid his tuition. Later, his fame as a fiction writer overshadowed his artistic ability that once was considered promising.

While a student at Hiram College, he served the Disciples of Christ Church and ultimately entered the ministry. The demands of college courses and church work became overwhelming to the young minister and he headed for the Ozark Mountains in southwest Missouri to regain his health. While recuperating he preached his first sermon in a log cabin school. This ecclesiastical experience convinced him that he could do more good and reach more people by preaching than in any other field. Consequently he later accepted pastorates in Kansas and Missouri and received a yearly salary of $400.

While a minister in Pittsburg, Kansas, he delivered a sermon-story portraying the many evils found in the town. His purpose was to arouse the congregation into action and to eliminate saloons and brothels. He read his story to parishioners in installments and they heartily endorsed his narrative, encouraging its circulation to a broader audience. Published as a novel entitled *The Printer of Udell's,* it appealed to thousands of readers and inspired Harold Bell Wright to continue writing.

In 1906, the sickly minister, his wife Frances and two sons Gilbert and Paul, returned to the Ozarks for an extended vacation of rest and meditation. He wrote *The Shepherd of the Hills,* a simple story regarded as a form of printed ministry filled with moral teachings. The book was a huge success and again he concluded he could reach more people with his writing than through his preaching. He began to travel in search of new information and collected local data to be used as background material for future stories. Although he kept busy with his writing career, he continued to work for his church.

In 1907, Wright accepted the pastorate of Redlands Christian Church and moved his wife and children to the small southern California community with prospects of improving his poor health in the milder climate. While in Redlands, he explored the nearby mountains and peaceful deserts and soon blended nature, religion and romance into his idyllic tales. After a short time, he resigned his Redlands pastorate and moved to the Imperial Valley to devote his energy to writing.

In the fall of 1909, he wrote of his personal observations of the desert and it was published as *The Calling of Dan Matthews*. His descriptive material had been carefully researched with the events of desert reclamation checked for inaccuracies by expert engineers. Perhaps his most famous story was *The Winning of Barbara Worth,* an epic dealing with the development of Imperial Valley. This literary sensation published in 1914 sold more than two million copies and became a successful moving picture starring Ronald Colman and Vilma Banky. The drama involved a dramatic struggle of man against nature and writing the gripping story took its toll on Harold Wright. He wrote the last few chapters while confined to bed and his ultimate recovery was a slow process.

One of the author's early visits to the Mission Inn took place on the Fourth of July 1912, a year after publication of *The Winning of Barbara Worth*. When he registered at the hotel he gave his occupation as an Imperial Valley rancher from El Centro. The Wrights had their third son, Norman Hall, by this time and the family no doubt came to the Mission Inn to celebrate the holiday and watch the fireworks at Lake Evans in Fairmount Park.

Wright purchased property in Arizona and built a simple ranch home in the remote desert where he could write without distractions. One day while horseback riding, he was struck by a car and suffered extensive injuries including a broken leg and damage to his chest and lungs. In 1915, he was confined to a Tucson hospital over the Christmas holidays. He ultimately contracted tuberculosis and to improve his health he resorted to living outdoors. He wore white clothing to protect him from the sun and set up a camp with a hooded desk to shade his eyes while writing. He lived in this outdoor environment called "Camp-Hole-In-The-Mountain." After some months he regained his health and completed a story called *When A Man's A Man* on April 30, 1916.

One year later Wright returned to the Mission Inn to celebrate Easter and attend the Easter Sunrise Service on Mount Rubidoux. Other celebrities were present in 1917 including the famous hometown opera star Marcella Craft and popular Wisconsin writer Zona Gale. Days before Easter, the United States declared war on Germany and consequently the service was noticeably subdued. The speakers remarks, nevertheless, appealed to Wright who later commented, "I was afraid the vast crowd might rob the service of its spiritual significance."

After Frances and Harold Wright were divorced in 1918, the writer moved into the Mission Inn and it was to become his home intermittently for the next several years. In February 1919, be began a new work of 90 thousand words entitled *The Re-Creation of Brian Kent,* unplugged his phone and allowed no interviews or unnecessary interruptions. The story set in the Ozark Mountains involved a young man who embezzles money from his employer to please his materialistic wife. Wright completed the last chapter at noon April 27, 1919 and immediately sent the manuscript to Chicago for publication.

The next day Riversiders filled the Loring Theater to see Harold Bell Wright in person and to see a ten-reel silent movie of his story *The Shepherd of the Hills.* Prior to the performance, the writer entertained the cast and production crew with a true Ozark dinner in the Mission Inn. They gathered in the Spanish Patio where long tables were covered in traditional red and white checkered table cloths and waitresses were dressed in Mother Hubbard calico outfits and braided hair.

The movie was advertised as the most entrancing love romance ever told – more than a masterpiece. Every seat in the Loring was occupied from the orchestra pit to the last row in the gallery. Theater seats cost 25 to 50 cents, plus War Tax even though World War I had ended. Riverside Mayor Horace Porter introduced Harold Bell Wright who explained to the audience that the movie had been shot in the San Fernando Valley under his supervision. He explained the picture was purely an attempt to relate a story without unnecessary spectacular photographic effects or drastic stunts. At the conclusion of the movie, the leading lady Cathrine Curtis and author Harold Wright were summoned to the stage to receive bouquets of flowers and a standing ovation.

On August 5, 1920, Harold Bell Wright married Mrs. Winifred Potter Duncan of Los Angeles. They lived in Redlands and Tucson where they maintained a luxurious Spanish hacienda on 160 acres of natural desert scarcely visible to the public. The house was decorated with Indian furnishings and works of art including handcrafted wooden carvings and wrought iron fixtures. Wright had supervised the simple interior decorating that included a large pleasant workroom with picture windows displaying the surrounding desert. The central patio, filled with native Arizona plants, had a colorful blue-green swimming pool and the beautiful desert home was frequently featured in home and garden magazines.

By the 1930s, Tucson had grown in size and extended to the Wright house, once eight miles from town. Trees and neighbors obstructed his desert view and Wright sold the property and purchased a home site in Escondido, 25 miles north of San Diego. They built their 'dream house' and called it *Quiet Hills Farm.* Growing fruits and vegetables and tending farm animals, however, did not improve Wright's health and he continued to deteriorate

Living closer to Riverside, the Wrights visited the Mission Inn and the Miller family more often. They were always welcomed and included in all social events at the hotel. The couple spent the winter of 1933 in the Inn and Alice Richardson invited them to join her for Thanksgiving dinner. It was a wonderful holiday and this became an annual custom for the Wrights.

Shortly before Harold Bell Wright died in 1944, he sold his farm and moved to San Diego. Although he had made many moves throughout his life he once commented, "I am fond of the Mission Inn and it feels like coming home to be there. One simply cannot estimate the value of intangible charm."

Chapter 20

HELEN ADAMS KELLER
1889-1968

Anne Sullivan Macey stepped onto Riverside's Loring Theater stage on March 13, 1914, and spoke to the attentive audience about her famous student, Helen Keller. Several hundred patrons filled the theater and every seat was occupied with extra chairs added in the aisles and on stage. Helen Keller, both deaf and blind, attracted the curious and sympathetic. Many came to learn how she managed to overcome such serious obstacles and observe her methods of communication. Her Riverside appearance attracted people from throughout the county, many of whom idolized the young woman who offered inspiration and hope to all handicapped people.

The program began with Mrs. Macey's recollections of her early years with her student who had lost her sight and hearing from a high fever when only 18 months old. The young, rebellious girl staged violent rages when she failed to get her own way or to be understood. The concerned Keller family made extensive inquiries in search of help for their daughter. Most doctors and informed authorities, including Alexander Graham Bell, recommended the Perkins Institute for the Blind in Boston.

Mrs. Macey continued her story recalling that she had completed a course at Perkins when Mr. Keller inquired about a teacher. Since she was the only student who could see well enough to make a trip alone to the Keller home in Alabama, she was hired as the six-year-old girl's governess and teacher. With no equipment and less hope she undertook the challenging task of educating the unruly youngster. She taught her student the hand-palm alphabet by the sense of touch with rewards of cake for correct answers. In no time she put words to objects such as water and food and soon mastered Braille. She could read by feeling raised dots that represented letters and that ability changed her life. Helen later learned to speak by feeling her teacher's throat and lips thus forming sounds to correspond to their placement. With great perseverance and a keen mind, 16 year-old Helen Keller entered Radcliffe College in 1904.

The presentation continued describing Helen's college career and her graduation with honors and Bachelor of Arts degree. Anne Macey admitted she had stayed with Helen through four years at Radcliffe and had devoted her life to her student's welfare. After college, Helen wrote a number of articles about her problems and those of other handicapped people in an effort to educate the public about the hazards of those less fortunate and to ask for their understanding. In spite of her efforts to become financially independent, the income from her publications did not cover her special needs and living expenses. The proud lady humbly accepted monthly donations from benevolent benefactors such as Mr. and Mrs. Andrew Carnegie.

In a concerted effort to become financially self-sufficient, teacher and student decided on a national lecture tour although Mrs. Macey realized that Helen could be difficult to understand at times. Nonetheless, she told the Loring audience, "We are on our first lecture tour of the United States and happy to be in Riverside this March 13, 1914." Then on cue, Helen's mother Kate Keller escorted her daughter on stage, avoiding the extra rows of chairs, and faced her towards the waiting audience. The 34-year old was dressed in a filmy white gown and her face was covered in a bright, pleasant smile. An instant hush swept through the theater when she first appeared and after she politely bowed and smiled, a loud round of applause echoed through the building. Miss Keller continued to smile at her invisible audience as long as she could feel vibrations through the floorboards of the stage.

The audience strained to hear her low voice and her inspirational comments were slowly and haltingly delivered. With a smile she said, "I find life good. I have happiness and contentment and thankfulness and I can sing *I Put My Trust In the Lord.* You do not begin to use all the wonderful gifts you are given. Believe more in your powers and use them to their full value and you will acquire much more." She closed her spiritual messages by explaining the calamity of the blind, though immense, did not take away the value of service, friendship, humor, imagination and wisdom. After 15 minutes, Helen Keller offered to answer any questions the audience might have. She placed her hand on Mrs. Macey's face and "listened" to her repeat the question and gave her answer promptly. The alertness and depth of her explanations astonished the audience and clearly revealed Miss Keller's sharp mind and keen intellect.

When the honored guest was asked her opinion of Riverside, she replied, "I thought it beautiful." And the logical next question was, "But how do you know it's beautiful?" Her quick return was, "By the smell." She could identify the fragrant scent of the navel orange blossoms enveloping the town. At the conclusion of the program, the three ladies were escorted to the Mission Inn where they spent a restful night.

The following day Helen Keller was unable to keep her scheduled appointments because of extreme fatigue. Before coming to Riverside, the ladies had been in Los Angeles where Miss Keller had experienced a small miracle when she "heard sounds" of grand opera. The Chicago Opera Company was in town and its star Madame Stevens offered to sing for the young lady and selected "Die Walkurie" in which A natural is reached and repeated several times. Helen Keller grew emotional when she withdrew her fingers from the singer's lips and raised her hand to her left ear. She insisted she heard sounds and described it as her idea of water falling from a height, a tinkling noise. A day later, Madame Stevens received a gorgeous basket of American Beauty roses and a note of gratitude. The note read, "We three women deeply regret we cannot see and hear you perform tonight for we have a lecture in Riverside. We send flowers, a wee tribute to the most beautiful voice I have ever heard." It was signed Helen Keller, Kate Keller and Anne Macey.

Daily travel and performances were difficult for Helen and illness or fatigue occasionally necessitated the cancellation of an appearance, including an honorary luncheon hosted by Riverside Girls High School. Much to their disappointment, the girls were denied the opportunity to see and hear the celebrated lady who had unintentionally created a minor Riverside controversy

Local newspapers reported pleasing stories about Helen Keller and her "happiness" speech. Words describing her beautiful philosophy of life, her radiant eloquence, and her smile like an apostle were most flattering but one paper's editorial disagreed with the general consensus. The article admired Helen Keller's perseverance and marveled at her achievements. "Somehow one in seeing and hearing her gets the impression that she is exhibiting not her hard won accomplishments of education and speech but rather the physical handicaps which made their mastery so difficult." The editor wanted to protect her from public displays and sympathetic audiences who felt pity for her. Needless to say, Helen Keller never read this editorial and her Riverside performance at the Loring Theater was a huge success breaking all box office records. More than 1100 people filled the theater with a seating capacity of only 840 and at least 300 people were turned away including 150 guests of the Mission Inn. One of the hotel guests was former vice-president of the United States Charles Fairbanks who couldn't get seats for his family. Local criticism did not affect Helen Keller's successful lecture series and the following year she returned to Riverside for another engagement.

On March 15, 1915, Miss Keller and Mrs. Macey appeared on the stage of the Loring Theater but this time they faced a much smaller audience. The program followed the previous format with Mrs. Macey describing her involvement in her student's life. Some believed Miss Keller's speech had improved from the year before but others did not. Many in the audience felt the well-rehearsed talk had too many trite spiritual and religious phrases but nevertheless she received a tremendous ovation and admirable praise.

The ladies stayed at the Mission Inn for several days where they headquartered while lecturing in Ontario and nearby communities. On St. Patrick's Day 1915, Frank Miller spent considerable time with the ladies and personally guided them around the Mission Inn. They visited the Presidential Suite, the Music Room, and the expansive Spanish Art Gallery. As they walked around the Court of the Birds they could smell the sweet fragrance coming from blossoms of the parent navel orange tree planted by President Theodore Roosevelt in 1903.

Three days later, on March 20, the city of Riverside celebrated Orange Day, an all day affair with a morning parade, speeches in White Park and athletic contests concluding with a street dance at night. Miss Keller and Mrs. Macey did not attend the activities and remained in their Mission Inn quarters planning their return home to Connecticut.

During the 1920s, Miss Keller became a highly paid celebrity and continued to appear coast to coast on the Orpheum vaudeville circuit. She also wrote magazine articles and published books about trials of the handicapped and contributed her proceeds to charities for the blind. In 1921, she organized the American Association of Workers for the Blind and worked to establish the American Foundation for the Blind.

Anne Sullivan Macey died in 1936 and Helen Keller was lost without her constant companion. Fortunately Polly Thomson, Keller's secretary, took on Anne Macey's work and the ladies lived comfortably in Easton, Connecticut. Motion pictures were based on Keller's life such as

The Unconquered and *The Miracle Worker.* Shortly before her 88th birthday, she died peacefully at home. The Keller Endowment Fund was her legacy to other handicapped people and her accomplishments were an inspiration to all people.

Mark Twain was a good friend and a close Connecticut neighbor. He once claimed, "The two most interesting characters in the nineteenth century were Napoleon and Helen Keller."

This interesting lady who toured the Mission Inn with Frank Miller often exclaimed, "It is very pleasant to live here in our beautiful world. I cannot see the lovely things with my eyes, but my mind can see them all, and I am overjoyed."

In March 1914, when Helen Keller visited the Mission Inn the hotel was filled with an assortment of diverse people, but the most conspicuous group had to be the athletes of the illustrious baseball team, the Chicago White Sox.

This double armed cross symbol was adopted by Elbert Hubbard's Roycroft Enterprises in 1900.

J.H. HALL COLLECTION

The Mission Inn Rain Cross insignia combines a double barred cross, an Indian rain symbol, with a Mission style bell and has become a Riverside community design.

J.H. HALL COLLECTION

Elbert Hubbard, founder of the Roycroft colony.

Elbert Hubbard and Frank Miller encouraged students at Sherman Institute to make Arts and Crafts style furniture.

This macaw derived his name from the bright blue features resembling Napoleon's uniforms.

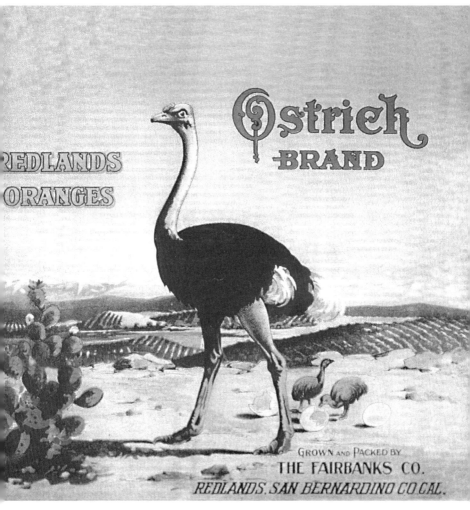

Vice president of the United States Charles Fairbanks and his son owned a citrus grove near Riverside and marketed their fruit under the Fairbanks label.

COURTESY OF FLOYD MCDONALD

The Presidential Suite occupied by Mrs. J.P. Morgan in 1910.

MISSION INN FOUNDATION – MUSEUM PHOTO

Frances Tracy Morgan, wife of the infamous New York banker.

Well-known author Harold Bell Wright periodically lived in the Mission Inn.

In 1911 Harold Bell Wright wrote the novel "The Winning of Barbara Worth" and she became a celebrity. The fictictious character even appeared on a Riverside citrus label.

*Helen Keller, on the left, is communicating by feeling
the lips of her teacher.*

Today a weathered commemorative plaque rests at the base of the White Sox Redwood Tree in Low Park.

J.H. HALL COLLECTION

Dewitt Hutchings and friend pose by the ancient Nanking Bell coveted by Louis Comfort Tiffany.

RLHRC Photo

In 1931 Tiffany's glass church windows were installed in the new St. Francis Chapel of the Mission Inn.

George Wong learned to cook in the Mission Inn and later opened the Bamboo Gardens Restaurant in Chinatown.

The sign reads:

COUNTY OF RIVERSIDE HISTORICAL MARKER

CHINATOWN

A 7-ACRE SETTLEMENT WAS FOUNDED HERE IN 1886 BY DUEY WO LUNG AND OTHER LEADERS OF RIVERSIDE'S PIONEER CHINESE. UNTIL 1900 THE POPULATION RARELY DROPPED BELOW 150 AND DURING THE CITRUS HARVEST OFTEN NUMBERED SEVERAL THOUSAND. THE BRICK BUILDING, ERECTED AFTER THE GREAT CHINATOWN FIRE OF JULY 31, 1893, IS THE LAST OF 26 ORIGINAL STRUCTURES ALONG CHINATOWN AVENUE.

A happy George Wong in 1968 when the County of Riverside recognized his Chinatown.

RLHRC Photo

LORING THEATRE

THURS. MAR. 2

ONE NIGHT at 8:20

First Appearance in the West in Several Years of
America's Foremost Actress

CHARLES FROHMAN

presents

Ethel Barrymore

In the play in which her triumph has been without
parallel in the history of the American stage

"DÉCLASSÉE"

by
ZOÉ AKINS

The Most Eagerly Awaited and Most Distinguished
Engagement of the Year

PRICES—BAL. $1.00, $1.50, $2.00—MAIN FLOOR $2.50
PLUS WAR TAX
Seats Now On Sale.   Phone 592

*Although World War I had ended before 1922, Riversiders paid a
War Tax to see America's Foremost Actress.*

Chapter 21

THE CHICAGO WHITE SOX
1914

In March 1914, Riverside baseball fans were thrilled to attend a major league game played in their own backyard. The Chicago White Sox of the American League agreed to play the Los Angeles Angels of the Pacific Coast League in an exhibition game at Evans Park. The Chamber of Commerce endorsed and promoted America's national sport and requested local businessmen to close their doors for business on that occasion. On March 11, between 2 and 4 o'clock, the town of Riverside was devoted exclusively to the exciting contest. Baseball fans had previously witnessed other big league games played in Riverside but this promised to be the greatest, with several nationally known athletes participating.

White Sox manager Billy Sullivan made reservations for 25 members of his organization to spend the night at the Mission Inn. The hotel was busy that spring with guests from throughout the nation including Charles Fairbanks of Indiana, former vice-president of the United States, who was enjoying an extended vacation at the Inn. In spite of the high occupancy, ample accommodations were provided for the White Sox. Spring training had brought the team to southern California where more moderate weather conditions enabled them to work out and hone their skills before their regular baseball season. The Chamber of Commerce had enticed the team to appear in Riverside after a satisfactory financial agreement had been reached. A large percentage of pre-season ticket sales and gate receipts went directly to the White Sox organization.

Before the big game on Wednesday the 11th, members of the Chicago team checked into the Mission Inn. The hotel provided a hearty meal for the hungry athletes. After lunch, the young men walked a block and a half to the nearby Young Men's Christian Association located on the northeast corner of Eighth and Lemon streets. The red brick building had enough lockers and showers to accommodate both ball teams. Players changed into their spotless uniforms before queuing up for their grand downtown parade and competitive ball game.

Crowds of spectators gathered around the YMCA building hoping to get a glimpse or possibly an autograph of a famous athlete. Glenn Calkins, a local car dealer, furnished 24 new Ford cars to convey the players and local dignitaries to the ballpark. Calkins had just opened a new Ford agency at Eighth and Lemon and was anxious to advertise his exclusive car dealership. A last minute addition to the caravan was Police Chief Corrington who jokingly commented that he was there to make sure none of the ball players were kidnapped during their stay in Riverside. The Sherman Indian Band led the parade of cars down Main Street where enthusiastic crowds applauded and cheered the teams as they passed by. Their snappy band music added to the excitement of the day as the well-known ball players waved and acknowledged the eager spectators lining the route. The parade went along Main Street to Fourteenth and then west to Brockton Avenue and finally to Evans Park.

Evans Park was named in honor Samuel Cary Evans, landowner and developer who had donated the ten-acre parcel to the Riverside School District in 1906. For the first few years the property was used for gardening by the students from nearby Grant School to give them a better understanding of the growing and cultivating of various crops. Sometime later an agreement was reached with Riverside's Park and Recreation Department whereby a portion of the property in the Tequesquite Arroyo was converted to a baseball field. And thus on March 11, 1914, Evans Park became the site of the big game between the Sox and Angels.

The grandstands were filled to capacity with anxious fans who paid "six bits" (75 cents) for a reserved seat in the bleachers. Although the crowd appeared to be large, the gate receipts were disappointing. Nevertheless, those who attended the big game had a great day of baseball. Riverside Mayor Oscar Ford threw out the first pitch and fans yelled with anticipation as the game began. They shouted themselves hoarse when a player on either side slammed a ball into a far corner of the field. A close call by the umpire drew even louder screams. Each team used two pitchers during the two-hour contest that featured wild pitches, double plays, base hits, and lots of free advice from the grandstand. The White Sox won the game 12 to 8 and both teams were grateful for the good workout and the enthusiastic fans. Accordingly, a rematch was scheduled within the next few weeks.

On March 25, the Chicago and Los Angeles teams returned for another game of baseball at Evans Park. However on this occasion there was less publicity. The Chamber of Commerce decided to include the players in its annual Arbor Day festivities, with representatives from each team participating in ceremonial tree planting prior to the game. Several of the White Sox placed a special commemorative redwood tree in the newly created Low Park. Located several miles south of the Mission Inn, it was named for Charles H. Low, the previous owner. Ironically, Low had made his fortune in Chicago before becoming a citrus grower in Riverside

White Sox first baseman Hal Chase was selected to take part in the Arbor Day ceremony primarily because he made his home in San Jose, California. He dug the hole while team captain and third baseman Harry Lord placed the redwood tree in the ground. Wives of the players were present and they proudly listened as Mayor Ford christened the tree the White Sox Redwood. The Riverside Monument Company designed an appropriate stone plaque that was placed at the base of the tree.

On the afternoon of March 25, the White Sox and Angeles played their second game at Evans Park. A small crowd of spectators watched as the Sox defeated the Angeles 19 to 5. Charles A. Comiskey, owner of the Chicago White Sox, expressed his appreciation for Riverside's interest in his ball team. Furthermore, he apologized for not attending the tree dedication and thanked the Chamber of Commerce and city officials for their efforts in support of the game of baseball.

Baseball fans throughout the United States followed the career of White Sox first baseman Hal Chase with great interest. The handsome young man was nicknamed "Prince Hal" and gained celebrity status as a smooth, graceful player with abundant natural ability. He executed double plays with perfection and seldom made an error. In 1919, following a noticeable increase in the number of errors committed by Prince Hal, rumors surfaced that he was wagering on baseball games and that the errors may not have been accidental.

Later that year, a Boston gambler furnished authorities with a signed affidavit alleging that Chase's miscues were deliberate and were intended to affect the outcome of the game. Furthermore, he produced a cancelled check, payable to and endorsed by Chase, in payment of a wager. With rumors and allegations confirmed, Chase quietly left baseball without fanfare or publicity. That same year the White Sox lost the World Series amid continuing rumors and were dubbed the Black Sox. Chase's misdeeds were not made public until 1920, when he was arrested at his home in San Jose. He was subpoenaed to Chicago where he testified at the trial of eight White Sox players accused of throwing the 1919 World Series. White Sox owner Charles Comiskey declared that although the players in question were subsequently acquitted for lack of evidence, they should be barred from baseball because of the damage they had done to the game. The American public soon forgot the scandal and focused on the 1921 World Series between the Yankees and Giants.

Riverside sports fans followed the big league players as well as the hometown boys who made it to the big time professional teams. One of the most unlikely candidates to become a famous player was a young man named Jack Meyers. This Mission Indian was born and reared in Riverside where he started playing ball in grammar school. When his father died, he had to work to support his mother, Felicite, who was employed by the Miller family as a housekeeper at the Glenwood Hotel. In 1904 he went to Arizona and New Mexico where he played baseball in the minor leagues. Because of his Indian heritage, his teammates fondly referred to him as Chief Meyers.

While in New Mexico, he learned of a scholarship at Dartmouth College exclusively available to American Indians. He discovered the English Earl of Dartmouth had given a large donation to be used for the education of American Indians and in return for his generous gift, the college was named for him. Jack Meyers took advantage of this peculiar opportunity, passed the entrance exam and became the first Indian to receive the Dartmouth scholarship. During his one year in college, Chief Meyers was treated as an honored guest with many invitations and a full social life. However, after a year, he decided to return to baseball where his athletic ability propelled him into the spotlight and national fame.

As a New York Giant, he became a famous pitcher, catcher, and hitter. He astonished the baseball world with his distinct talents and local residents were proud of their hometown boy. Through the years there have been many well-known local ball players. Most recently Bobby Bonds and Dusty Baker became important sports figures who began their careers at Evans Park when they were in grammar school.

As the years passed, the triangular shaped property known as Low Park was planted with a variety of trees. In 1927, several notable authors who were staying at the Mission Inn were asked to participate in a special tree planting ceremony. Authors Zona Gale and Joseph Lincoln planted coco palm trees in a section of the park designated as Friendship Grove. Most of the trees were planted as a memorial or remembrance to honor distinguished citizens. Appropriate plaques, embedded at the base of each one, once stated the name of the honoree and the date it was dedicated. Unfortunately most of the plaques have disappeared. However, the White Sox Redwood Tree and stone plaque can still be seen in Low Park, a reminder of an Arbor Day event that took place decades ago.

Chapter 22

THE MAYO BROTHERS
William James 1861-1939 -Charles Horace 1865-1939

During the 1914 Christmas holidays, a limousine transported ten carefree tourists from Pasadena to Riverside for a day of sightseeing and lunch at the popular Mission Inn. Dr. William Mayo, eldest of the celebrated brothers of the Mayo Clinic in Rochester, Minnesota, was one of the travelers. He commented to reporters that his California vacation had no professional purpose and he was merely visiting good friends and relaxing after the growth and expansion of his medical clinic

Recently the Mayo brothers, Will and Charles, had consolidated their scattered offices, remote laboratories and medical facilities into one major structure. It had taken more than two years of planning and, after the final dedication of the Mayo Clinic, Dr. Will was in need of rest and decided to spend the holidays in southern California. Charles Loring, his close Minnesota friend, insisted that he visit Riverside's Mission Inn and its owner, Frank Miller. The Lorings had spent many winters at the Inn and considered it a second home. On December 30, the famous surgeon toured Riverside and the Mission Inn and met Frank Miller.

Dr. Will was delighted with every aspect of the hotel and candidly admitted he had never seen such a beautiful and unique place in all his travels. He was intrigued with the tall, thin palm trees entwined with small Christmas lights and took special interest in the new Spanish Art Gallery about to open the following night. Dr. Will Mayo and his friends had an enjoyable lunch in the California Dining Room of the Inn and promised to return someday and "stay for a indefinite period."

Will Mayo's life had been dedicated to his medical practice and continuing education with little time remaining for recreation and pleasurable travel. Will and Charles were introduced to the challenge of medicine at an early age by their father, Dr. William W. Mayo. As youngsters, their father had taken them on house calls and let the boys help in minor operations in his office. The brothers attended Rochester Central School where they befriended classmates Bert and Fred Younglove.The Younglove family later moved to Riverside where they became community leaders and successful businessmen. Will Mayo continued his education at the University of Michigan earning a doctor's degree and in 1883 practiced medicine with his father in Rochester. In the meantime, Charles enrolled at Northwestern University and in 1888 he received his medical degree.

The Mayo brothers worked together at St. Mary's Catholic Hospital where the Sisters of St. Francis provided excellent nursing care. They initiated office visits in place of time consuming house calls and developed specialized departments and improved procedures with centralized equipment and machinery. They started the practice of using antiseptic and rubber gloves during operations to reduce infections and due to these extra precautions, most serious cases were assigned to them. To eliminate confusion about whose patient waited in an examining room, colored paper was placed above the door frames – red for Dr. Charles and green for Dr. Will. They each performed thousands of operations, worked long hours and gained national recognition for their successful treatments. Doctors came from around the world to observe their surgical skills and new techniques. In September 1911, Dr. Hugh R. Martin of Riverside spent several weeks in Rochester studying at the Mayo Clinic to learn new methods to benefit his patients.

Dr. Will was the businessman of the two who looked to the future and planned in advance. He became famous for his gallstone operations and cancer treatments while Dr. Charles specialized in goiter and thyroid disorders. Patients of Dr. Charles compared him to the personable cowboy Will Rogers because of his friendly repartee. Although the brothers had distinct personalities, their lives were intertwined in a number of ways. Their families lived next door to one another, they owned country cabins side by side and the families maintained one common bank account. Will and Charles were often compared to identical twins because they chose to combine their daily lives into a simple existence.

As long as they both lived they continued their studies and to learn of new medical procedures, improved methods of treatment and different theories. They frequently traveled to Europe and investigated new procedures, often thought to be revolutionary. The Mayo brothers finally began to realize financial benefits from their hard work and limited their practices to diagnosis only. The brothers excelled in recognizing disease symptoms and their treatments usually resulted in a patient's improvement. They made their diagnosis available to everyone by charging patients according to their ability to pay. In addition they shared their knowledge with others and became proficient teachers and lecturers.

After some years the 1914 Mayo Clinic grew obsolete and, despite additions, extra space was rented in nearby offices. The sprawling clinic became one of Frank Miller's destinations in 1923 when he and his wife Marion traveled east to inspect a variety of hospitals. The three-month trip was primarily a vacation for the Millers who were nevertheless searching for suitable designs that could be used in Riverside's future community hospital. While in Rochester they visited Florence Loring, widow of Charles Loring who had died the year before. When Frank Miller appeared fatigued, Florence suggested a complete physical exam at the nearby Mayo Clinic where doctors found nothing physically wrong with Miller other than a nervous condition. It was suggested that this could account for his slight depression and the doctors prescribed complete rest with no thoughts of business or the management of the Mission Inn. Albert Miller, Frank's nephew, had been promoted to assistant manager of the hotel, working with his Aunt Alice Richardson ensuring that Frank Miller's business was in good hands. While recuperating at the clinic, he befriended Will and Charles Mayo and invited them to stay at the Inn whenever they came to California. Several weeks later, Frank and Marion Miller left Rochester and continued their vacation, visiting friends and relatives and observing various hospitals along their route.

As word spread of the success of the Mayo Clinic, rumors soon followed claiming surgical miracles by its founders that ranged from the ridiculous to the sublime. Dr. Will is said to have replaced the stomach of his brother with that of a sheep and Dr. Charles reportedly returned the compliment with a calf's liver for Dr. Will. These fantasies and others including transplants from elk and moose abounded and were promptly disavowed by the Clinic. Many people thought the Mayo brothers could do anything with the human body.

In 1928, a new Mayo Clinic building was dedicated and it soon contained the latest hospital equipment and a good, capable staff. The 15-story structure became a Rochester landmark and the Mayo Clinic gained international fame as the best diagnostic center to be found anywhere. When the doctors reached their sixties, they decided to leave the clinic and the practice of medicine. Dr. Will retired in 1928 and Dr. Charles in 1930, allowing the brothers to travel together for the first time. One of them had always remained in charge of the hospital while the other traveled on lecture tours or to attend professional meetings. Now the brothers had the finances and time to enjoy life and they began spending milder winters in Arizona. The warm climate was pleasing and they purchased adjoining winter homes in Tucson.

The Mayo brothers were extremely popular personalities and at one time were asked to run for Congress. The doctors had started practicing medicine at a transitional period of change and their innovative ideas were effectively used and achieved national acclaim and acceptance. In spite of their tremendous contributions to the medical profession, some still thought the publicity they generated was unethical advertising. Professional men did not advertise publicly at that time and such practices were frowned upon. Writers, most often unqualified in medical matters, frequently misquoted the Mayos and serious misunderstandings resulted among doctors. Nonetheless, the brothers gained great prestige and public affection from the thousands of people they helped.

In March 1936, Dr. William and Charles Mayo and wives drove from Rochester, Minnesota, to Pasadena, California. They were anxious to leave the eastern weather where in Iowa they had encountered ten-foot deep snowdrifts. When they arrived in Arizona and southern California they were greeted with mild spring temperatures. The couples came west to attend meetings and clinics in Los Angeles, San Diego and San Francisco and along their route they stopped in Riverside for a short visit. Frank Miller had died the previous year at the age of 78 and they wanted to pay their respects to Alice Richardson.

A local newspaper reporter interviewed the noted surgeons during their brief Mission Inn visit. Dr. Charles stated, "We are here at the Inn to renew our friendship with Mrs. Alice Richardson, sister of Frank Miller, former master of your famous hostelry. While Mrs. Richardson has greeted us with the same hospitality, we miss our old friend Frank Miller who made this Inn famous over the entire world. We miss his friendly and neighborly handshake. Riverside must miss Mr. Miller who had done so much for your city,"

Dr. Will inquired about the Younglove family who had moved to Riverside many years before and was informed that Norton Younglove, the father, had become a horticulturist with a home and citrus grove on Brockton Avenue. Bert, now known as Albert had successfully developed a one man operation, selling coal oil house to house into a thriving business called the Home Oil Company. Fred, was now a respected retail businessman, president and general manager of Rouse's, Riverside's oldest and finest department store. The Mayo brothers were told members of the Younglove family continued to serve the community.

When the doctors said good-bye to Alice Richardson they expressed their gratitude and desire to return for a longer visit. Will and Charles Mayo died just two months apart in 1939. They left a valuable legacy to the medical profession but, unfortunately, could not spare the time to enjoy the restful atmosphere of the Mission Inn, the exact medicine they had prescribed for their former patient, Frank Miller.

Chapter 23

LOUIS COMFORT TIFFANY
1848-1933

Louis Tiffany created several works of art, including his pictorial window, *The Bathers,* for the 1915 San Francisco Panama-Pacific Exposition. Although some of his work received gold medals for their craftsmanship and aesthetic beauty, the temperamental artist had withdrawn the window following a disagreement with management over its placement. His subsequent travels in California, while obscured by his obsession for privacy, ultimately led him to Riverside. When Tiffany arrived at the Mission Inn, several attendants including his own chef accompanied him. The eccentric artist rebuffed Frank Miller's warm greeting and offers of special service and informed him there was no need for further communication. This was to become the beginning of an unpleasant experience for Frank Miller.

Tiffany dined occasionally in the pleasant California Dining Room where his attendant placed screens around his table to shield him from other diner's curious stares. Privacy screens were not unusual in Riverside hotels when guests wished to consume alcoholic beverages with their meals without scrutiny or criticism. In 1916, four Riverside hotels renewed their table liquor permits issued by the city council and the Tetley, Reynolds, Holyrood and Mission Inn hotels continued to serve alcohol under a city ordinance.

Upon his departure Mr. Tiffany asked to speak with Frank Miller regarding the purchase of the giant bell standing near the entrance to the lobby. The Nanking Bell was actually a Chinese gong acquired through an agent in 1914 after its discovery in a demolished temple. The bell, seven feet tall weighing two tons, was the largest in Miller's extensive bell collection. Smaller, less historic bells could be purchased as souvenirs in the hotel's gift store but Frank Miller was adamant about retaining this particular one. While Louis Tiffany sat impatiently in his chauffeured car, he made one last attempt to buy the unusual bell when he told Miller to set his own price. The artist was again informed that the Nanking Bell was not for sale so he immediately left Riverside. The Tiffany bell episode was recorded in Frank Miller's 1935 reminiscences for his biographer Zona Gale.

The aristocratic attitude of Louis Tiffany was a natural trait, having been born into wealth and privilege. His father, Charles Lewis Tiffany, owned the prestigious New York silver and jewelry store, Tiffany & Company. Young Louis attended private schools but rejected a university education and a position in his father's business to pursue his interest in art. After he graduated from school at the age of 17, he studied with several New York artists before going to Paris where he became a student of Leon Bailly. He traveled, studied and learned the techniques of painting with oils and watercolors. Most of his early works depicted romantic scenes in exotic places and many were displayed in American galleries and international art shows. His watercolors were often oriental designs with landscaped gardens and peaceful surroundings. While in Europe he became intrigued with colored glass windows found in ancient churches and old monasteries.

Tiffany returned to New York, established a glassmaking plant and after many experiments, developed a process to produce iridescent, stain textured glass called Favrile. This amazing glass reflected true colors and depths of texture that he incorporated into artistic, useful household items. Tiffany products rapidly became popular especially his leaded-glass lampshade with small pieces of colored glass arranged in staggering tiers. With the increased use of electricity, the Tiffany lamp was considered utilitarian as well as decorative.

Tiffany held scheduled exhibitions in his New York studio where he displayed original stained glass, mosaic windows and decorative screens. Reproductions of the originals on display were made available to various commercial users including hotels, theaters, churches and libraries. His church windows frequently differed from the traditional and depicted nature, such as flowers, birds and insects, with biblical characters. Tiffany's popular dragonfly design used art glass and glass jewels in a hand-leaded inset pattern.

During the 1880s and 1890s, architects often blended different styles and building materials to create mansions for wealthy eastern families. Extravagant interior detailing was believed to reflect the financial status of the owner and Tiffany catered to this clientele. Many mansions were filled with non-functional bric-a-brac. The prominent New York architect Stanford White often worked with Louis Tiffany and the men developed a close relationship in their business and social lives. In 1882, Charles Tiffany commissioned White to design a single building for his family, encompassing three separate residences, a six-story structure at 72 Street and Madison Avenue. After three years of construction, Charles Tiffany retained the first two floors, his daughter and her family moved into the third floor residence and Louis and family occupied the fourth floor. The top floor, with skylights and a high ceiling became Louis Tiffany's studio.

The entire building resembled a Swiss Chalet covered in thin, flat bricks that became known as Tiffany bricks. Due to its immense size, high turret and steep, black tile roof, it appeared more like a commercial building. An arched driveway opened from the street into a landscaped interior courtyard with individual staircases leading to each private residence. Although Louis Tiffany acquired other houses later, he considered this one his home until he died. Ironically, the wealthy Charles Tiffany never occupied the house. When he died in 1902, he left the property plus an inheritance of three million dollars to his son Louis.

In 1903, Stanford White and Louis Tiffany were commissioned to design and decorate a new church for Dr. Charles Henry Parkhurst, a controversial New York preacher. His sermons took issue with the city's political, economic and social policies and New York officials became his bitter enemies. Dr. Parkhurst was labeled both a hypocrite and a welcome messenger of change but nevertheless continued to fill his church with devoted followers. The new Madison Square Presbyterian Church at Fifth Street and Madison Avenue was dedicated in 1906 and was regarded as Stanford White's most beautiful building. Tiffany designed mosaic windows, small and large, for the church and its glass-domed ceiling allowed sunlight to reflect on the colored pieces of glass. Unfortunately the building was destined to be sacrificed by encroaching skyscrapers and in 1919 the Metropolitan Life Insurance Company acquired the property. Most of the ornamental materials in the interior and exterior were recycled or incorporated in other local churches, museums and buildings. Tiffany reclaimed at least eight of his artistic stained glass windows, three transparent, three opaque and two circular.

These windows were no doubt stored in Tiffany's Oyster Bay home, Laurelton Hall. In 1919 he established a foundation on this property as a summer retreat for aspiring artists. Laurelton Hall housed much of

Tiffany's fine art work where it was accessible to students in a museum-like setting. He designed the commercial appearing structure without the assistance of a professional architect and the three-story clock tower building became his part time residence.

In 1923 Frank Miller and his wife Marion left Riverside for a three-month vacation with their final destination New York City. While in New York, the Millers stopped at Tiffany's Jewelers to shop for a small souvenir. Louis Tiffany discovered the Millers were in town and invited them for lunch at his home Laurelton Hall. There these two men negotiated an unknown transaction whereby Frank Miller came into possession of eight Tiffany windows saved from the Madison Square Presbyterian Church.

Upon Frank Miller's return to Riverside, he told newspaper reporters, "It is quite marvelous that this talented artist was able to incorporate his wonderful ancient style art in these windows that will harmonize perfectly with our Mission Gothic architecture. They are the most valuable examples of Tiffany's remarkable work."

Frank Miller sent his friend and architect Arthur Benton to New York to supervise dismantling and packing of the valuable Tiffany windows. The first shipment of six 7 x 16 foot windows was painstakingly taken apart, piece by piece, and placed in crates for transportation cross-country. The jewel-like pieces of Favril glass were packed separately from the intricate metal framework. When the well-packed shipment arrived safely in Riverside in June 1924, Miller hired three experts from the Charles E. Clifford Company of Los Angeles to assemble one window. In a hotel room on the second floor, west of the Spanish Art Gallery, J. S. Melville of the Clifford Company reconstructed the window. He was considered a skillful artisan having previously worked in New York with Louis Comfort Tiffany for over eight years. He claimed the windows were among the finest in the world, each designed and painstakingly created by chipping old glass. He predicted when they were installed it would be possible to see the exquisite tones of color that exist in each and every piece of glass.

The ultimate disposition of these six windows and the additional two rose windows finally took place in 1930 when the St. Francis Chapel was constructed. The last wing addition to the Inn was the International Rotunda begun in June 1929 and completed in the fall of 1931. The beautiful St. Francis Chapel houses a hand-craved, golden altar built in Mexico in the 1740s and seven Favrile glass windows created by Louis Comfort Tiffany. Six tall Tiffany windows were installed along opposite walls in the chapel with three iridescent on the north and three transparent on the south side. The windows depict symbols of different seasons of the year and contrasting biblical scenes. Inset above the tall entrance door to the chapel is one of the Tiffany circular windows with the inscription "Hast Thou Made Them All." The other one is incased in the west wall of the Galeria, an adjoining room used for banquets.

This wedding chapel reflects Tiffany's artistic ability and remarkable talent for blending nature and religion into unforgettable art forms. These eight spectacular Tiffany windows continue to be preserved and protected in Riverside's Mission Inn.

About the time Louis Tiffany left the Mission Inn with his chauffeur and other attendants, another eccentric character named George Wong entered the hotel through the back door.

Chapter 24

GEORGE WONG
1900-1974

George Wong, the last resident in Riverside's once bustling Chinatown was perhaps the best known and most likeable local character of his time. Easily recognizable, his winning smile exposed large white teeth and reduced his inquisitive eyes to little more than slits. He spoke broken English, frequently stuttered and although difficult to understand at times, managed to become the best-informed gossip in town. Because of his staid Oriental manner and pleasing personality, many residents of the community befriended him including the Frank Miller family. George had been an employee of the Mission Inn at various times and often passed through its doors, most often the tradesman entrance.

Born Wong Ho Leum in China, he came to Riverside in 1914 and lived with the S. Leonard Herrick family who gave him the name, George. The teenager lived with the Herricks for a number of years and attended school where he learned the language of his new country. His parents, born in San Francisco, had returned to China where they had three children including George. The father, known as Little Joe, later decided to return to America but his wife chose to stay in China and remained there the rest of her life.

When 14-year-old George Wong arrived in Riverside, Chinatown was a colony of hard-working men and a fluctuating population. During the orange harvest there could be well over a thousand workers living in the small shacks and shops. The workers labored from sunup to sundown in the orange groves and vegetable gardens and as laundrymen or domestic help. Chinatown, located near Tequesquite Avenue, was near the Santa Ana River that furnished water to adjacent Chinese vegetable gardens. George Wong's father, Little Joe, leased a small plot of land and grew a variety of vegetables that he sold house to house from his horse and wagon.

During World War I, George Wong was in high school and worked briefly in the kitchen at the Mission Inn. Most employable young men had been drafted and Frank Miller was in need of hotel workers. Young

Wong learned to cook in the well-equipped kitchen and without some basic food ingredients due to the war, cooking became a genuine challenge. He soon learned the art of improvisation and the techniques of preparing a variety of meals for numerous diners. Many years later, a mature Wong claimed he received a valuable and useful education as a kitchen helper and expressed his graditute to Frank Miller, his former employer.

On April 29, 1917, organized crime struck Riverside's Chinatown when three unidentified Chinese men shot the owner of Wong Fook's Noodle House. The assassins had entered the shop and ordered their noodles and while being served, promptly fired one shot at Fook. He struggled to the door but after a volley of shots he died and the three men escaped through the Brockton Avenue door to a waiting car. California's tong war had claimed a Riverside victim and residents of Chinatown feared for their lives. Within the Chinese community, elders were looked upon to judge and punish wrong doers for minor offenses, but premeditated murder quickly caught the attention of the Riverside Police.

Police feared another such incident might occur and thus enforced a 6 p.m. curfew on stores and restaurants in Chinatown. Chinese tongs, unlawful secret alliances, were fighting among themselves throughout the state and George Wong soon learned the code of silence exercised by Chinatown residents. Twenty years after Wong Fook's death, his remains were placed in a small box and sent to a Hong Kong hospital to be claimed by relatives. It was a custom to return departed Chinese to their native homeland following interment of at least ten years in this country.

After Little Joe died in the 1920s, George Wong moved into Chinatown where only a few elderly men remained. Wong became the spokesperson for his countrymen and subsequently acquired the title of Mayor of Chinatown. A number of small shops still existed and townspeople patronized them for novelty items. Once a year its main street was filled with crowds of local people who came to observe and celebrate Chinese New Year. There were fireworks and merchants distributed trays of dried fruit and Chinese candy. Children long remembered visiting Chinatown on this festive occasion as it was generally off limits to them because of the proliferation of drugs and cigarettes.

The mystique of Chinatown triggered stories of hidden tunnels with secret passages beneath the buildings and the evil things that took place.

Chinese lottery flourished year round and it was rumored that opium could easily be obtained. Federal law enforcement agents investigated the site, believing it to be a drop for drugs originating in Mexico for distribution in Los Angeles. When George Wong was a student at Riverside City College, the sheriff's deputies kept him under surveillance on suspicion of selling drugs and concerned citizens wanted him arrested. In response to the rumors and public concerns, Wong was arrested. After a federal trial in Los Angeles he was acquitted of the charges but the stigma of this offense remained with him forever.

During the 1920s, Frank Miller built an elaborate summer home, *Villa Rockledge,* in Laguna Beach for his second wife Marion. Architect Arthur Benton designed the elaborate house built along a cliff overlooking the ocean. The tiled roof bungalow with a sturdy rock foundation took several years to build and Wong helped, proving to be a strong, dependable worker and reliable handyman. Since Frank Miller didn't drive, he occasionally hired George Wong to take him to Laguna Beach. The two-hour trip through the Santa Ana Canyon was a picturesque drive with citrus groves on either side of the road bordered in huge eucalyptus trees. Wong was not a good driver and he was constantly involved in accidents. Nevertheless, Frank Miller may have been oblivious to his driving ability and no doubt enjoyed George Wong's latest Riverside gossip.

When the last store in Chinatown closed in 1938, a few men remained while others moved to northern California to seek employment. In 1941, George Wong purchased the Chinatown property consisting of five acres with several old brick buildings. Many unanswered questions remain as to how he obtained this property but he nevertheless became the legal owner of Chinatown and this became his home.

Wong opened a Chinese restaurant called the Bamboo Gardens that faced Brockton Avenue. He claimed he couldn't make any money from it – "about two bits a month," – and added he couldn't support a wife and never did marry. During World War II, his restaurant closed and he went back to work in the Mission Inn kitchen. At the time workers were difficult to find due to military and defense plant demands for most employable people. The Mission Inn operated at maximum capacity and George Wong worked in a variety of jobs, primarily in the kitchen preparing meals for hundreds of servicemen and their families.

After the war, aging George Wong became somewhat of a recluse and moved into a travel trailer on his property. He lived there quietly, surrounded by weeds and mounds of dumped fill dirt where chickens wandered over piles of junk. Besides providing a good meal now and then, the chickens served as noisy lookouts. Wong began allowing people to store their cars on his property and soon more cars were added, many abandoned. He purchased old, used cars mostly owned by those who had been good to him as a youth, such as the Herrick family. Into this jungle of automobiles came wrecked and lifeless cars, many without traceable license plates or any means of identification. In 1954, the Riverside City Council instructed firemen to clear Chinatown because of the number of complaints concerning its appearance and possible health hazards. Although George Wong was notified numerous times of the violation, the property remained untouched. As firemen burned piles of accumulated trash, a grinning George Wong watched without comment or protest as his land was cleared of debris. The next day a new mound started taking shape.

In 1961, in spite of his unorthodox ways, the Riverside City Council named a new street Wong Way in honor of Chinatown's last resident. The two-way street connects Pine and Palm Avenue and is impossible to travel "the wrong way." George Wong died quietly in January 1974 from complications of pneumonia. His will named attorneys Russell Waite, a former grammar school friend, and Enos Reid executors of his estate. After a simple, short graveside service, George Wong was buried in Evergreen Cemetery overlooking old Chinatown and not far from Frank Miller's final resting place.

Although Riverside police patrolled Chinatown after George Wong's death to defer vandals and thieves, collectable items continued to disappear. Several arrests were made when merchandise and fixtures were found missing and tighter patrols increased. In August 1974, a Los Angeles firm announced a public auction would be held to dispose of George Wong's Chinatown collections. His estate was bequeathed to his sister, Wong Ping Siem in China or, if deceased, to her son. There were many legal issues concerning the inheritance of Chinese citizens but nevertheless proceeds from the estate were transferred to a bank in Hong Kong.

The five acre parcel was valued at $199,000; however, the amount of the actual sale is unknown. There were 98 old cars, mostly filled with old newspapers and debris. Several Franklin touring cars and a Rolls Royce Roadster caused quite a flurry of excitement because of the value of their scarce auto parts needed for restoration of vintage cars. The Riverside Municipal Museum became the recipient of bric-a-brac, ceramic jugs and medicine bottles found in Chinatown. At the conclusion of the two-day auction, George Wong's estate realized $360,000. A variety of expenses amounting to over $57,000 included inheritance and back taxes.

Officers of a Hong Kong bank representing Wong Ping Siem received a check for $78,468 but it is unknown if she claimed her brother's estate. As in life George Wong continues to be a local legend, a mysterious smiling man who passed through the back doors of the Mission Inn.

Chapter 25

ETHEL BARRYMORE
1879-1959

The celebrated actress Ethel Barrymore came to Riverside in February 1922 to perform in three one-night engagements scheduled in San Bernardino, Redlands and Riverside. She headquartered at the Mission Inn during her Citrus Belt appearances starring in the successful stage play *Declassee*. The famous star admitted, "I have always wanted to come to this beautiful hotel and city. This is the first opportunity I have had to make it possible. Many of my friends have spoken so highly of the Inn and Riverside." Ethel Barrymore had a strict policy of not giving personal interviews and it was quite a concession for her to make a statement to a local newspaper reporter.

One of her notable successes was her lead role *Declassee,* in which she portrayed a fictitious aristocratic English socialite, Helen Haden. The dictionary defines the word declassee as "one fallen or lowered to an inferior status" and that was to be the fate of the main character. The well-known actress had starred in the role since 1919 and the success of the stage play was attributable to her many years in England as a prominent socialite.

Ethel was born into the famous Barrymore dynasty and was destined to follow her famous father, Maurice, and grandfather, John Drew, as a performer. At age 17, with little more than a carpetbag of possessions and a letter of introduction, she went to England to accept a role in a minor British stage play. During the Victorian era in England, legitimate stage personalities enjoyed a unique relationship with high society and members of royalty. When the young and beautiful Ethel Barrymore appeared on the British stage, she attracted considerable attention and captivated many affluent and influential people.

Because of her sharp wit and intense intellect, she endeared herself to both men and women of all ages. She attended numerous social functions, often three or four a day, and her popularity grew as she charmed members of the royal family and their circle of friends. When she attended Queen Victoria's Jubilee Garden Party, admirers were more interested in the charming actress than the performance at the royal extravaganza.

Ethel Barrymore became a theatrical idol symbolizing the glamour of the theater and at the same time gained an honorable, prestigious social position achieved by few American women.

While pursuing a stage career in England, many unfounded rumors were circulated alleging her involvements with various suitors, including 28-year-old Winston Churchill. He was infatuated with the 23-year-old beauty who was full of life and ambition and after a persistent courtship he proposed to her in 1902. In spite of her great admiration for the promising young politician, she declined his offer in favor of her desire to continue her career in the theater. Determined to change her mind, Churchill hosted a dinner party in her honor and invited personal friends and distinguished guests to extol his virtues. His efforts were in vain, however, and the strong-willed actress remained determined to perform on the stage in the tradition of her family. Nevertheless, Ethel Barrymore and Winston Churchill remained lifelong friends and admirers.

The attractive actress once commented that she and her brothers "became actors not because they wanted to go on stage but because it was the thing they could do best." Ethel and her brothers, Lionel and John, were born into the respected Barrymore-Drew clan of renowned theatrical performers. The Barrymore family acquired the unofficial title of The Royal Family of the American Theater and represented the grandest traditions of their profession. Grandmother of the Barrymore siblings was Louisa Land Drew, one of the most respected and successful actresses in the nineteenth century. She married a well-known actor, John Drew, and their daughter Georgiana also chose a career on the stage. Georgiana Drew married a young English actor originally named Herbert Blythe who had changed his name to Maurice Barrymore. The talented couple became parents of the famous Barrymore children, Lionel, Ethel and John. Actor Maurice and actress Georgiana were continually on tour and either enrolled their children in private schools or left them with their grandmother, Louisa Drew. Grandmother Drew had retired from the stage but pursued another career as booking agent and theater manager. She had great influence in American stage productions and ambitious performers cultivated her friendship. This was advantageous for 12-year-old Ethel who appeared on stage for the first time when she substituted for an actress suddenly taken ill. Although her reviews were mixed, she had launched a theatrical career that ultimately brought her fame and fortune.

Regardless of the lack of family stability, Ethel and her brothers displayed a close relationship throughout their lives and carried on several family traditions. On opening night of a new play, they would each present their starring sibling a big, red apple signifying "speak your piece and get a reward."Another tradition established by Ethel Barrymore began one night early in her career after endless curtain calls. In order to quell the enthusiastic audience, she candidly remarked "That's all, there isn't anymore." This spontaneous comment became her personal signature whenever there was an abundance of curtain calls.

Although Ethel Barrymore appeared on stage for many years, she remained a beautiful woman for her age. Women throughout the country attempted to imitate her appearance, dress, coiffure and gracious manners. She was an inspiration to a society that was seeking dignity and culture as well as adventure and humor. Her following included women of all ages and whenever her photo appeared in newspapers or magazines, her current hair-do was immediately adopted by hundreds of admirers. The idol of the stage became the idol of American women.

At the age of 30, Ethel Barrymore married Russell Griswold Colt whose grandfather, Samuel Colt, invented the six-shooter, repeating revolver. Her father-in-law headed the prestigious United States Steel Company and he purchased an impressive, large house in Manaroneck, New York, for the newlyweds.Ultimately Ethel and Russell Colt had three children, Samuel, Ethel and John. After 14 years of marriage, the couple divorced. Ethel remained unmarried because of her Catholic upbringing in convent schools.

In 1922, Ethel Barrymore was experiencing financial problems resulting from her separation and ultimate divorce. Back taxes, debts and over-spending prompted her return to the stage in order to satisfy mounting debts. Her western tour was well advertised and theaters sold out wherever she appeared. Audiences adored her and eagerly awaited the opportunity to see the charming member of the royal theatrical family. On March 1, Ethel Barrymore, and a cast of 40, appeared at the Redlands Wyatt Theater and every seat was taken.The stunning actress wore a large assortment of gowns and received many curtain calls. Although she presented her lines flawlessly, some believed she did not live up to previous performances.

When the heavy stage curtain went up in Riverside's Loring Theater on

March 2, every seat was again occupied despite previous engagements in San Bernardino and Redlands. Many theatergoers, nevertheless, came from surrounding communities to see the famous star in one of her celebrated plays.

The Riverside Enterprise reviewed Miss Barrymore's performance and stated she appeared her best as an English matron in the unusual story. She portrayed a high society woman who falls from grace and the resulting emotions of lost status creates the drama. The newspaper stated, "Her role combined comedy with serious moments of matrimonial disaster. The unfolding story was so skillfully presented that Miss Barrymore received unexpected curtain calls at the end of the second and third acts."

The great lady left Riverside the day following her performance in the Loring Theater and townspeople hoped she had departed before reading the review of her play in *The Riverside Daily Press*. Newspaper reporter, Polly Playgoer apparently did not like the play nor Miss Barrymore's performance and her newspaper review declared the evening a great disappointment. Furthermore, she claimed Miss Barrymore failed to establish her character as a magnetic personality of British aristocracy. The reviewer felt the leading actress gave a poor performance but wrote that the cast played their part in holding the story together. Polly Playgoer's final, stinging insult, "A large audience paid the usual compliment of applause to the artist." No doubt that is why the critic never used her true name.

Ethel Barrymore continued her tour of the play *Declassee* and played to capacity audiences in theaters throughout southern California. Devoted admirers gladly paid a dollar or two, plus a war tax even though the war had ended, to see "their Ethel" in person. During the 1920s and 1930s, this multi-talented lady produced and directed a number of successful Broadway stage plays. In addition she could sing and her sentimental songs with a touch of whimsical humor delighted her devoted public. In 1928, she opened the Ethel Barrymore Theater in New York City and successfully appeared in *The Kingdom of God*. She was devoted to the stage for many years and offered acting opportunities and encouragement to aspiring young actors.

In 1931, Ethel Barrymore appeared in a successful revival of *The School for Scandal* in the Ethel Barrymore Theater. After several seasons of mediocre stage roles, her performance in this stage drama was hailed as one of her finest. The period costumes revealed her stunning figure and her poise and sweeping carriage set the right dramatic mood for the story. Her most famous stage role, however, was considered to be Miss Moffat in *The Corn Is Green* which opened in New York in 1940 and enjoyed a three-year run of 477 performances. Ethel Barrymore was then considered to be at the peak of her talents, vital and idolized. Meanwhile, her brothers were leading men in a number of diverse stage plays. Lionel directed and acted in motion pictures and was also an artist and composer. John played Shakespearean roles and appeared on stage, screen, and radio.

Ethel Barrymore's outstanding career encompassed radio, television and motion pictures. On her 70th birthday, August 16, 1949, a nationwide radio program paid homage to the popular actress who represented the highest traditions of the theatrical world. Both she and her multi-talented family entertained the American public for several generations, but it was a 43-year-old stately actresses named Ethel who provided a memorable evening to hundreds of appreciative theatergoers in Riverside, California, in 1922.

Chapter 26

GRAND DUKE ALEXANDER MILHAILOVICH
1867-1933

Before World War II, members of nobility and royalty frequently passed through the doors of the Mission Inn. Countesses, Earls, Ladies and Sirs and countless Viscounts and Lords made their presence known when they visited the Inn. One of the most likeable titled personalities, however, was the enchanting Grand Duke Alexander of Russia. He arrived in Riverside on March 21, 1930, accompanied by his secretary Arkady Roumanoff, after traveling from San Francisco to Los Angeles on the scenic *Sunset Limited*. Known as a notable writer and public speaker, the Grand Duke was touring the United States and Canada to stimulate interest in the disastrous plight of his beloved Russia. His lectures were based on his personal experiences and observations.

As the guest of Frank Miller, the Duke occupied the grandest apartment in the Mission Inn, the Alhambra Suite. Located on the top floor of the hotel, it overlooked the Spanish Patio and inner courtyard. The two-room apartment, originally named the Alhambra Mirador in 1928, included a balcony with wrought-iron railing and a beautiful landscaped courtyard. The interior was finished in rich Mexican cedar with hand-carved beam ceilings in the sitting room and bedroom. A large, antique framed fireplace and pleasing furniture provided comfortable surroundings. The Alhambra Suite provided the desired privacy requested by the Grand Duke. After the visitors settled into their spacious suite, they reorganized their busy itinerary. They expected to stay in southern California for ten days before continuing their tour in New York.

The following day, Allis Hutchings escorted the visitors on a personal tour of the hotel that started in the Court of the Birds and featured a spacious garden filled with colorful spring flowers. The pergolas over the walkways were covered with flowering wild grapevines and the rose garden flourished with perfectly shaped buds of every color and fragrance. Allis Hutchings took the guests to the Music Room, considered one of the most striking features of the Inn. With its elevated stage, gigantic pipe organ and rows of chairs, the room was available for musicals, conventions, dances and lectures. Choir stalls lining the walls were copies of Westminster Abbey seats and the mahogany parquet floor resembled tiled pavement found in Europe. With a tall, heavy beam ceiling, antique furnishings and walls covered with banners, national emblems and flags, the huge room resembled a banquet hall found in a Spanish castle. Some guests believed the national emblems represented Frank Miller's awareness of international unity and his effort to prevent world conflict. The Grand Duke was pleased with the international theme because his first lecture was to take place in the Music Room.

His Imperial Highness was the scheduled Sunday evening speaker at the weekly Song Service held in the Music room. These lectures were open to holders of Song Service cards, as well as members of Riverside's Peace Conference and local educators. Topics covered diverse subjects centered on current events and were presented by noted speakers and educators. Grand Duke Alexander Milhailovich was indeed an important lecturer whose impressive pedigree embraced the Romanov lineage, the early imperial family that ruled Russia from 1613 to 1917. The late Czar Nicholas II was his close friend and brother-in-law and King George of England was his cousin. He had married the Czar's sister, Grand Duchess Alexandrovna, and their family included three children. Grand Duke Alexander was the heir to the Russian throne if the royal dynasty had been reinstated.

On Sunday evening, March 22, Arthur Wheelock, superintendent of Riverside schools, introduced the Grand Duke to an enthusiastic audience assembled in the Music Room. The tall, handsome 63-year-old gentleman appeared aristocratic with a neatly trimmed goatee and pointed mustache. He spoke English in a very cultured manner although his distinct Russian accent made it difficult for some to understand. Nonetheless, he began by sharing childhood memories of growing up in Russia where he learned to respect and admire nature. This compelling interest kept him from embracing any single form of religion and he frequently doubted traditional religious doctrines. Because of his royal heritage and prestigious station in life, he was expected to pursue a military career. Ultimately he rose in rank to command the Russian naval aviation corps and became a highly respected officer.

In 1893, he visited the United States for the first time and became intrigued with the great energy and diverse accomplishments of the American people. He shared with the audience that his three sons were working in New York and he believed they were obtaining the best education possible. He said his wife, the Grand Duchess, was a guest of King George and Queen Mary at Windsor Castle during his tour of the United States. Alexander gave an account of his country's sad state of affairs and sought the understanding and cooperation of the world.

He recalled that when Czar Nicholas II ascended to the throne he was only 27 and confided to him the great burden of leading 200 million people. He claimed the Russo-Japanese War had been forced upon Nicholas who had been ill advised. "We did not need any more land and it was an unhappy war for us," the Grand Duke said. Russia was not prepared for war and it was well known that Nicholas lacked the confidence of his countrymen and was not a strong leader. Nicholas was forced to give up his throne in 1917 to a provisional government and subsequently the Bolsheviks took over. Dolefully, the Grand Duke recalled that after Nicolas had abdicated, he was imprisoned and on July 18, 1918, he and his family were executed. Alexander took the position that Nicholas should not have abdicated and was naive to think he was dealing with honorable people.

He said, "I had everything in life that is supposed to give happiness to mortals -wealth, riches, power. I lost it all in the revolution but I did not lose my soul. The material can be taken from you, but not the spiritual." When his friends and relatives were murdered, the Grand Duke sought refuge in the Crimea and his life was spared only because of the sympathy of an unknown officer. Alexander continued, "The people who started the revolution did not know Russia or its needs. They made false promises of freedom but Bolshevism transferred people into the worst kind of slavery. The Bolsheviks seemed to hypnotize the Russian people and I don't understand it."

The Grand Duke's idealist solution to his country's upheaval revolved around the doctrine of love and the sanctity of family and property that would ultimately lead to a prosperous nation. He added that he was opposed to physical intervention and favored moral intervention through the teachings of Christ. He further stated the political objective of the Bolsheviks was to overthrow capitalism by force. In 1919, this movement was renamed the Communist Party. Regardless of past events, the Grand Duke's message of love and compassion for a peaceful world was the primary theme of his lectures and presentations.

The Grand Duke had a full schedule of engagements throughout southern California. Monday morning he reiterated his personal theory of spiritual unity to students gathered in the ivy-covered chapel at the University of Redlands. In the evening, he was again on the stage of the Mission Inn's Music Room speaking to members of the local Present Day Club. Early Wednesday morning he and his secretary drove to Los Angeles where the Grand Duke addressed a Breakfast Club and later that afternoon appeared before the student body at the University of Southern California.

His lecture was scheduled so those students studying international relations and political science could attend as a class project. The vice-president of the university introduced the Grand Duke who addressed a large audience of students and faculty He recalled details of the revolution and preached his theory of love. "Love of neighbors, love of humanity, love of everything living. In Russia there is hatred, immorality and common property and no religion." He reminded the students that the United States is the financial and economic power of the world and he hoped it would also become the spiritual power. At the conclusion of his lecture, a Russian tenor sang two solos followed by a luncheon honoring Grand Duke Alexander. In spite of his busy schedule, he graciously agreed to participate in a ceremonial tree-planting event before leaving Riverside.

On March 28, members of Riverside's Beautification Committee gathered in Low Park in a section known as Friendship Grove. Friendship Grove accommodated trees previously planted by well-known writers Henry Van Dyke, Zona Gale and Joseph Lincoln and other distinguished visitors. When the Grand Duke planted a cocos plumosis palm tree committee members were grateful for such a lasting reminder of his visit. In response, he expressed hope that love and peace would flourish as well as the tree. One of the many important people present at the ceremony was V.D. Starosselsky, a former general in the Imperial Russian Army, who lived near Riverside.

Grand Duke Alexander Milhailovich and his secretary left Riverside and continued their scheduled tour to his final lecture in New York City where the two men visited old acquaintances from Russia now living in America. Before returning home to France, the Duke made several final appearances in the big city. One evening while ascending steps to a platform on a ballroom stage, he missed his footing, slipped and fell, injuring his spine. The unfortunate accident resulted in a serious sprain and back pain that confined him to bed. When his injury became acute he moved from Paris to a small village near Menton to rest and recuperate. Despite his serious back problems he often talked of returning to America and referred to it as "my second homeland." His condition deteriorated, however, and the Grand Duke died of his spinal injuries in February 1933, three years after his Riverside visit.

Riversiders were saddened to read of his death and fondly remembered the proud, dignified gentleman who sought to help his country regain its standing in a civilized world. They recalled his visit and speculated that there was a strong probability that had he lived, he would have returned to Riverside and the Mission Inn. A month after the Grand Duke left the Mission Inn in 1930, another auspicious guest arrived who also believed in spiritual dedication. He was Heber Grant, president of one of the largest church congregations in the world.

Chapter 27

HEBER JEDEDIAH GRANT
1856-1945

On Saturday April 20, 1930, President Heber Grant, his family and church officials arrived at the Mission Inn as guests of Frank Miller. As the seventh president of the Church of Jesus Christ of Latter Day Saints, Grant was also the prophet seer and revelator to thousands of Mormon disciples throughout the world. His brief visit coincided with Easter weekend, the busiest time of year for Riverside and the hotel. Although every room was occupied, Frank Miller extended every courtesy to the distinguished Mormon visitors.

President Grant had a full schedule of church activities yet he graciously accepted Miller's invitation to attend the traditional sunrise service on Mount Rubidoux. Guests, including songwriter Carrie Jacobs Bond, were awakened before daylight on Easter morning by the carillon chimes. Frank Miller provided touring cars to transport visitors to the summit of the mountain where they gathered at the foot of a tall wooden cross. The 15-foot high redwood cross was dedicated in 1907 to honor Father Junipero Serra, founder of the California Missions. The 22nd annual sunrise service featured Dewitt Hutchings recitation of Henry Van Dyke's poem, *God of the Open Air.*

After the morning activities a local newspaper reporter interviewed President Grant regarding his impressions of the mountain top service. Grant stated, "I consider myself fortunate that I was in Riverside at Easter time. It was all so unusual, beautiful beyond words. My journey to dedicate the local branch of our church proved timely, and, as a guest of Frank Miller, I was privileged to hear this historic and memorable service."

President Grant was in Riverside to formally dedicate a new church located on the northeast corner of Third and Locust streets. Although the church had been in operation six months, it had not been officially dedicated until the head of the church could participate in the ceremony. A branch of the California Mission (Latter Day Saints) had been established for Riverside Mormons in 1925 and shortly thereafter members made plans to build a local chapel. A building permit was issued in 1928 for a one and one half-story building to be constructed by Charles J. Hannah at an estimated cost of $19,000.

The architecture was described as "classic Spanish, clean Italian and modified Mediterranean." With rough stucco walls and a tile roof, it was constructed of reinforced concrete, steel frame windows and built to last indefinitely. Although there was seating capacity for 300, accommodations for additional members could be provided by the addition of chairs in the balcony and choir section. The basement, designed as a recreational hall, contained a fully equipped kitchen, a stage, and seven classrooms. When the church was completed it had cost $47,000, with the parent Salt Lake church contributing $18,000.

On Easter Sunday afternoon, President Grant formally dedicated the Riverside Church of Jesus Christ of Latter Day Saints. The 300-member congregation had paid for all costs of construction and furnishing and the church was free of debt. As the guest speaker, President Grant traced the history of the Mormon Church and how its influence had extended around the world. He related some of the hardships encountered by early pioneers and many in the audience remembered that nearby San Bernardino had been settled by Mormons.

In 1850, after the Mormon settlement was established in Utah, a new wagon route to the Pacific Coast became necessary. Several routes were considered and individual parties were sent to uncharted territories to establish convenient supply stations along the way. One immigrant party of 150 wagons traveled through the Mojave Desert to the San Bernardino Rancho owned by the Lugo family. The Mormons obtained 80,000 acres of land in 1851 and quickly organized the San Bernardino "stake" of the Church of Jesus Christ of Latter Day Saints. The name San Bernardino, in reference to the Lugo land grant, was given to the Mormon town and plotted as a one-mile square. Some descendents of the original Mormon families who had settled in San Bernardino were present for President Heber Grant's dedication of the Riverside church.

President Grant had previously visited San Bernardino when he dedicated a small chapel that had formerly been the Old Ninth Street School. In February 1922, the building was completely remodeled into a convenient church facility. Although the town once had a substantial number of faithful members, the Mormon population had long since been depleted. In 1852, President Brigham Young proclaimed plural marriage an integral part of the Latter Day Saints doctrine and urged the faithful to practice polygamy. As a result the following years were filled with hostility towards them and in 1858 church members were instructed to return to Utah and unite. The town of San Bernardino reduced in size as the faithful departed. It was during these years of turmoil that the future president of the church, Heber Grant, was born.

His parents, Jedediah M. Grant and his sixth wife were loyal Mormons who practiced polygamy. Jedediah had marched with Brigham Young from Illinois to Utah and became a pioneer of Zion. He named his son Heber in honor of President Young's best friend and advisor, Heber Kimball. When Salt Lake City incorporated in 1851, Jedediah Grant served as mayor until his early death at the age of 40.

Young Heber grew up with few advantages and joined the church before he was 20 years old. As a devout member he later was elected into the higher echelon of the Council of Twelve. His business interests involved insurance companies and accordingly he organized the Utah Home Fire Insurance Company, thereby earning a reputation as an astute businessman. During these years he had three wives and fathered nine daughters and two sons. In 1890 when the Mormon Church prohibited the practice of polygamy, he followed the accepted doctrine of monogamy.

When Utah was granted statehood in 1896, Heber Grant was an established business executive and staunch member of the Latter Day Saints. As a result he was sent to Japan in 1901 entrusted with the establishment of the Mormon doctrine. He engaged in missionary work there for several years and later traveled through Europe for the same purpose, all with notable success. His accomplishments soon reached the church hierarchy in Salt Lake City and in 1916, President Joseph F. Smith appointed Heber Grant head of the Council of Twelve, a select group of men who supervised church affairs.

President Smith was a frequent early visitor to California, often as a missionary en route to the South Pacific Islands, by way of San Bernardino. On later visits, after he had ascended to the presidency, he traveled in private Pullman cars, owned by the Mormon Church and reserved for the use of dignitaries. He was well received throughout the state, including Los Angeles where he was the guest of the exclusive Jonathan Club. In 1913, the church purchased a home in Santa Monica for Grant's use during Utah's harsh winter seasons that he enjoyed until the property was sold in 1923.

After the death of President Joseph Smith, 62-year-old Grant was elected to the presidency on November 23, 1918 – the most prestigious and esteemed position in the Mormon Church. *The Associated Press* sent night wires to major cities reporting — "Heber J. Grant Takes Mormon Church Reins" and he immediately appointed his two counselors, Anthony Lund and Charles Pearose. The tall, bespectacled and bearded Grant became the leader of the Mormon Church including all stakes, wards, missions and branches.

During his long presidency, Heber Grant frequently visited California for both business and pleasure and became widely known and respected throughout the state. Because he was a keen judge of character and shrewd businessman, he earned a small fortune in the insurance business. In spite of his successful career, he never lost sight of his childhood poverty and his followers regarded him as an excellent role model.

Heber Grant was a strong leader and during the great depression in the 1930s, he adhered to and strictly enforced the church doctrine on welfare. Although mindful that many of the faithful would no doubt be among the unemployed, he admonished them not to accept government relief unless they gave a full day of labor in return. As an alternative, he formulated a plan whereby the church provided work for its members, with wages often in the form of food or other daily necessities. Grant inspired his followers and ultimately many found unique solutions to their depression-related problems. They pooled their resources and bartered or exchanged services with one another. The novel idea of self-sufficiency in time of need was well received throughout the nation by Mormons and non-Mormons alike.

In 1934, novelist Upton Sinclair became a candidate for governor of California. Although primarily a fiction writer, he had become outspoken on social issues and advocated a government program known as EPIC, Eliminate Poverty in California, to solve the ills of the depression. Many people favored his views and the promise of better days to come. However, President Grant strongly opposed the program claiming it a government handout and urged church members to vote for Sinclair's opponent. His opinions were widely publicized and may have influenced Sinclair's defeat.

Frank Miller admired Heber Grant's leadership qualities and his position on self-reliance. The two men were a year apart in age and each manifested a pioneer spirit of independence. They both believed in hard work, were respected businessmen and adamant pacifists. The walls in Frank Miller's office were covered with photos of his friends and those he admired including Heber Grant, the sixth president of the Church of Jesus Christ of Latter Day Saints.

When Heber Grant died on May 12, 1945, he was characterized as one of "those unusual men of the world, a man who always did what he thought was right." Twelve thousand church members viewed his body and funeral services in the historic Salt Lake City Tabernacle were broadcast to thousands more who thronged the temple grounds. He was considered a pioneer of self-reliance and a significant influence on the growth of the west.

In April 1930, another visitor to the Mission Inn was a likeable, down-to-earth cowboy named Will Rogers who entertained the American public for years.

Chapter 28

WILLIAM PENN ADAIR ROGERS
1879-1935

When cowboy-philosopher Will Rogers performed at the Riverside Municipal Auditorium in April 1930, he entertained a full house with timely observations of everything under the sun. Admirers from throughout southern California sought tickets for the show and it sold out quickly. The bowlegged, gum-chewing actor was the star of a Junior Aid fundraising program to benefit their civic projects. The organization, comprised of young women volunteers, affiliated with the Association of Junior Leagues of America in 1962. Will Rogers' radio and motion picture commitments made his personal appearances scarce and his performance in Riverside was quite an event.

The wisecracking comedian opened the show with a commentary on women's outrageous fashions and men's sacred service clubs. As a part of his routine he referred to his Indian heritage, noting his father's one-eighth and his mother's one-quarter Cherokee blood, after which he would remark, "My ancestors didn't come over on the Mayflower but they met'em at the boat." Everyone roared at his quick wit and down to earth philosophy and the evening was considered a great success with the Junior Aid realizing $255. Will Rogers spent the night at the Mission Inn and the next morning returned to his ranch in Santa Monica and his stable of horses.

The loveable actor was reared on his father's 60,000-acre ranch in Oklahoma where he developed a passion for horses. He spent his youth on the back of a horse and later as an adult commented that there was something wrong with a man that "don't like a horse." He not only learned to ride but also he mastered the techniques of roping. At the age of 23, he joined *Texas Jack's Circus and Wild West Show* and was billed as the *Cherokee Kid*. In weathered chaps, boots, and a large brimmed Stetson hat he twirled a lariat and skillfully lassoed moving objects with little effort. Spectators were amazed at his expert dexterity and quick reactions as he calmly chewed gum and innocently stared at the audience.

In 1904, Will Rogers participated in the St. Louis World's Fair, entertaining audiences with his intricate rope tricks. With this national exposure, his popularity increased and he joined a vaudeville troupe and performed at Madison Square Garden in New York City. By 1915, Rogers was a feature attraction and he signed a lucrative contract with the Ziegfeld Follies in which he shared billing with promising stars and gorgeous showgirls. On one occasion the theater manager was standing in the wings and overheard an exchange of wisecracks between Will Rogers and a member of the cast. As a result, the humorist was encouraged to talk to his audience while continuing to twist and twirl his ropes. His first conversation on stage brought down the house and he quickly developed confidence that encouraged him to ramble on about everyday subjects in his calm, folksy manner. He often repeated his favorite expressions, one of which was, "Swinging a rope is okay if your neck ain't in it." Many of his down-to- earth sayings have become American folklore, passed on from generation to generation.

Soon after the introduction of his talking routine, Rogers concluded that while audiences never seemed to tire of the chorus line, his subject matter would need to be changed on a daily basis to hold their attention. As an avid newspaper reader, it was no problem for him to keep up with political and national affairs as well as the people in the news and this became the source of his material. His timely quips of politicians and others of prominence made the news and he soon gained international fame, appearing in London, Berlin and Paris.

In 1918, the entertainer moved his family to southern California and started working in motion pictures. He purchased property in Santa Monica, built a comfortable ranch house filled with western mementos, planted hundreds of eucalyptus trees and developed two polo fields. He introduced the game of polo to his Hollywood friends and often recalled first playing the game in Riverside. The Riverside Polo Club maintained a race track and polo field at Chemawa Park where they held tournaments with clubs throughout California. The game of "hockey-on-horseback," also known as polo, utilized mallets and a ball the size of a baseball. Rogers organized many matches played on his Santa Monica property and gave credit to Riverside as the home of polo in California.

The comedian actor appeared in more than 70 motion pictures and made the transition from silent slapstick to talking dramas with little effort. He played roles that did not require the use of violence and never used tobacco or alcohol on screen. One of his expressions stated, "I've knocked around the world and although I was born and grew up on a cow pony, I prefer to travel in a Pullman. I can shoot pretty straight, but I've got no notches on my gun." Visitors to the Fox Studio lot always asked to see Will Rogers first and he was rated as the most popular performer in the country. A syndicated newspaper asked him to write a daily column and his brief commentary was subsequently circulated in over 500 papers across the country. His comments were condensed in a small box on the front page entitled "Will Rogers Says." He traveled often and played more benefit shows than any other Hollywood star and his byline enabled readers to follow his activities. In March 1928, the *Riverside Daily Press* began printing his timely observations and they were frequently quoted by teachers, ministers and businessmen.

In 1933, the Fox Film Company came to Riverside to shoot a picture entitled *State Fair* starring Will Rogers and Janet Gaynor. The cast stayed at the Mission Inn. Many scenes were filmed at the Southern California Fair Grounds near Fairmount Park with its sizeable racetrack and large grandstand. Motion picture companies often used this location to simulate background scenes for county fairs and horse races. Will Rogers played the part of a farmer who specialized in hog raising and the story revolved around competitive prizes. The picture was a success and Rogers said, "The movies is the grandest show business I know anything about. It's the only place where an actor can act and at the same time sit down in front and clap for himself."

The following year in 1934, Fox pictures returned to Riverside to shoot another movie at the fair grounds entitled *David Harum* starring Will Rogers. The famous actress Louise Dresser played his sister in a story about a horse trader at an 1893 county fair. More than a hundred local people were hired as extras, dressed in period costumes, and seated in the grandstand as spectators waving banners, eating popcorn, holding balloons and enthusiastically cheering at the horse races as a ten-piece band played.

On January 19, Will Rogers invited a Riverside writer and good friend, Ann Cameron, to visit the movie set at the fair grounds. The two had become friends when one of Cameron's stories was made into a movie starring Rogers. It was first released as *Green Dice* and later renamed *Mr. Skitch* but the final production was a disappointment to both the actor and writer. Rogers said he would like to remake the picture someday and follow Ann Cameron's original story, however, because of his busy schedule this did not happen.

That night at 11 o'clock Will Rogers was awakened by a phone call from the *Associated Press*. The actor had been suggested as a possible candidate for governor of California and the reporter wanted to know if he would throw his hat in the ring. His quick response was simple and to the point; "I'm not a candidate for nothing. I'd rather be a poor actor than a poor governor. I'd not get out of bed at 11 o'clock to take the oath of office."

While Will Rogers was in Riverside he continued to play nightly benefits in Santa Ana and nearby communities. At the same time he continued to write his January newspaper comments with the byline Riverside, California. One evening, he and Louise Dresser attended the Fox Theater to see the movie *Flying Down To Rio*. After spending five days at the Mission Inn, Will Rogers returned to his Santa Monica ranch.

The Fox Film Company issued a news item disclosing that they had spent over $8,000 in Riverside during the filming of *David Harum*. They claimed the stated amount didn't include personal expenses of the cast and crew and altogether the estimated expenses came to over $10,000. City officials and businessmen eagerly made necessary concessions to attract motion picture companies. In addition to financial gains, the city received favorable publicity for its important tourist industry.

After Will Rogers returned home, he wrote an unusual commentary about the Mission Inn. "It is the most unique hotel in America. It's a monastery, a museum, a fine hotel, a home, a boardinghouse, a mission, an art gallery and an aviator's shrine. It combines the best features of all of the above. If you are ever in any part of California, don't miss this famous Mission Inn in Riverside."

Will Rogers kept busy making motion pictures, writing books and articles and his daily commentaries during the great 1930s depression. He provided advice and told people not to gamble and wrote, "Take your savings and buy some good stock and hold it till it goes up, then sell it. If it don't go up, don't buy it." When someone asked him where he found his timely jokes, he answered, "Well, I just watch the government and report the facts, that is all I do and I don't even find it necessary to exaggerate." Another time he was asked about his knowledge of European royalty and said, "The old dukes and duchesses can converse in a lot of languages, but they're not strong on making a living in any of them."

Kings, diplomats, peasants and cowboys were friends of Will Rogers. He traveled the world and became known as the Ambassador of Good Will and was the guest of honor in many foreign nations. He preferred to travel by air and he possessed a special pass that entitled him to fly in airmail planes wherever he desired. He promoted aviation during his radio broadcasts and related his wonderful flying experiences. Ironically, Will Rogers was killed in 1935 in a plane crash in Alaska, but long before he died, he wrote his own obituary.

"When I die my epitaph or whatever you call those signs on gravestones, is going to read, I joked about every prominent man of my time, but I never met a man I didn't like. I am proud of that. I can hardly wait to die so it can be carved. And when you come around to my grave, you'll find me sitting there proudly reading it."

Chapter 29

ALBERT EINSTEIN
1879-1955

In 1930, Professor Albert Einstein and his wife Elsa accepted an invitation from the California Institute of Technology in Pasadena to be their guests for three months. The renowned scientist was given the opportunity to continue his research and to hold seminars explaining his scientific theories. He agreed to travel from Germany to California only if he could remain incognito and avoid crowds of curious people and well wishers. Einstein had gained international fame since receiving the prestigious Nobel Prize in 1922 for his theory of relativity. Wherever he appeared reporters and photographers followed his every move.

According to his wishes, travel plans were made to conceal his identity and officials booked passage under assumed names. Government approval had been obtained allowing the Einsteins to disembark before their ship docked in New York where J. P Morgan's private yacht would convey them to a secret retreat. Special arrangements were made with the Southern Pacific Railroad to provide a private Pullman car to convey the couple to California. When Professor Einstein was informed of these plans, he cabled officials at Caltech to cancel his travel plans as he had made other arrangements

Einstein had booked passage on the ship *Belgenland* to New York where he was to remain on board until it resumed its journey through the Panama Canal. On December 31, 1930, the *Belgenland* docked in San Diego and was greeted by crowds of curious people who had come to welcome the Einsteins. Evidently the popular scientist could not keep a secret and had informed the Jewish Telegraph Agency of his trip and itinerary. His daily routine continued to make world news and reporters chronicled his trip to the United States. Despite the attention he generated, a smiling Einstein appeared to enjoy his celebrity status.

After landing in San Diego some of the passengers commented that the Einsteins had kept mostly to themselves during the voyage but were "charming and gracious" whenever present. Eleven passengers from New York had made previous reservations to spend New Year's Eve at the Mission Inn and, after saying farewell to the Einsteins, they departed for Riverside. That night the gala party featured wandering troubadours, a dance band and no alcohol. The New Yorkers were amazed that no one at the party carried a hip flask, a common sight in their hometown. Several newspapers reported erroneously that Albert and Elsa Einstein spent New Year's Eve at the Mission Inn when in reality they were greeted and entertained elsewhere

After disembarking in San Diego, Einstein was the honored guest at a luncheon in the Grant Hotel. Henry Robinson, chairman of Security First National Bank in Los Angeles, then drove the visitors to Pasadena taking the scenic coast highway route through picturesque beach communities. They made a brief stop in Santa Ana and an Orange County newspaper reported that the most famous man in the world had stopped there. The Einsteins spent New Year's Eve as honored guests of Caltech officials and expressed their desire to see the colorful Rose Parade.

Elsa and Albert Einstein viewed the 42nd Rose Parade from the Security First National Bank executive offices that overlooked the parade route. They were served fresh orange juice and tea biscuits and the happy Professor puffed on his slim wooden pipe and chattered away in German. It was a joyous day for the Einsteins before commencing their obligations at Caltech.

The couple and their secretaries were provided lodgings in a seven-room bungalow located half a mile from campus. Einstein's daily life took on a routine similar to that of a post-graduate student as he studied, lectured and exchanged ideas with other scientists. He rode a bicycle to the Institute and after a long workday, played his violin for relaxation and enjoyment. Elsa, always the devoted wife, organized his daily activities and became his spokesperson. She could speak more fluent English and her husband felt more comfortable speaking German. Elsa, a blue-eyed, blonde with a substantial figure, possessed a likeable and caring personality and she fussed over her famous husband's health and well being.

After several busy weeks and a demanding schedule, Albert Einstein fell ill with a bad cold. When the couple received a generous invitation from Samuel Untermyer, a wealthy New York banker, to spend three days in the desert, they readily accepted. Untermyer's winter house was a spacious Italian styled villa built in 1927 with sweeping terraces overlooking the peaceful Coachella Valley. Elsa thought the dry desert air would benefit her husband and a three-day vacation away from work was most welcome. This short excursion also made news and an unfounded rumor surfaced that the Einsteins might stop at the Mission Inn for lunch on their way to the desert. Dozens of people gathered around the Inn for hours hoping to see Albert Einstein in person but to no avail. It was determined later that his driver had turned on the wrong road and ended up in Grand Terrace where he asked directions to Coachella Valley. While there he filled up with fuel and purchased a bag of local navel oranges they all enjoyed en route to the desert.

After three restful days, the Einsteins were driven back to Pasadena and on route they suddenly and impulsively headed for Riverside and the Mission Inn. Some of their traveling companions on the *Belgenland* may have told them about the wonderful hotel that was filled with beautiful objects. On the afternoon of January 27, 1931, the Einsteins appeared in the Court of the Birds. The short, bushy-haired Professor however seemed reluctant to enter the lobby. It was later learned he feared his presence might cause a commotion among hotel guests and he didn't want to upset them. Nevertheless, several bellmen noticed the couple's hesitation and instinctively escorted them inside to the privacy of the Presidential Suite where the doors were politely closed to the public.

Due to their unscheduled arrival there was no one in the Miller family present that day. Afternoon tea was offered to the guests and the Professor replied in English, "No tea, no tea - - water." A broad smile crossed his face when a large tray of water glasses and a pitcher of water arrived. Several newspaper reporters appeared after they had been informed of the unexpected arrival of such distinguished guests. They did not attempt to interview the Einsteins but instead joined their brief tour of the hotel. At one point Elsa Einstein looked confused and asked a reporter, "Was this ever a convent?" She was told it had always been a hotel and had been designed to resemble the architecture of early California Missions. The 55-year-old German lady seemed puzzled with this statement and no doubt had little knowledge of California history. During their tour, they discovered that the northwest corner of the Mission Inn property was blocked off due to construction of the International Rotunda. This six-story addition included the St. Francis Chapel, Galeria, and a central courtyard surrounded by a spiral staircase leading to businesses and offices.

Following the tour the Einsteins departed through the Court of the

Birds and stopped to admire the landscaped grounds. They paused in front of Allis and Dewitt Hutchings apartment where high in a tree above them sat Joseph, the bright red and gold pet macaw belonging to the Miller family. Aging Joseph had become a demanding, mean, old bird and few employees wished to care for him. The long-tailed macaw squawked at the departing guests and Albert Einstein came closer to get a better look at his brilliant colored feathers.

Bellman John Allen obligingly produced a long pole and transferred the noisy bird from the treetop to the Professor's arm. Elsa Einstein instantly disapproved of the bird so close and pulled on her husband's sleeve, urging him to get rid of the bird. Her smiling husband who seemed to enjoy the bird's presence ignored her protective, maternal poking. Joseph however became upset standing on an arm that was moving back and forth causing his footing to be unsteady. In self-defense the bird struck the closest object and pecked one of the Professor's fingers. John Allen immediately retrieved Joseph and placed him on a branch high in the tree.

Everyone fussed over Albert Einstein and his injured finger even though the skin was not broken. Apparently the bird had merely pinched the skin; however, the inquisitive Professor was unable to play his violin for several days. Hotel employees apologized for Joseph's bad manners and blamed the incident on his old age. Einstein was very gracious and took the unfortunate episode with a big smile and an understanding attitude. Upon departing the celebrated couple told reporters they hoped to return to the Mission Inn when they could spend more time but they were uncertain when that would happen.

When they returned to their Pasadena cottage they resumed their daily routine. Each morning he walked, or rode his bicycle, along the tree-lined streets to Caltech. If there were no seminars that day, he occupied a cell-like office in the ancient building known as the Norman Bridge Laboratory of Physics where he would write and study. Invariably he went home for lunch, always prepared by Elsa who did all the cooking. They received many social invitations but limited them to three a week. For weekend diversions, they took brief sightseeing trips around southern California and enjoyed the pleasant winter weather of the desert. Elsa Einstein discovered the beauty of Indian baskets and treasured her handcrafted gifts.

In February 1931, the Professor was invited by the Riverside Chamber of Commerce to plant a commemorative tree in Friendship Grove at Low Park. Other famous visitors to Riverside had been so honored including Grand Duke Alexander of Russia the most recent. Time, however, did not permit Albert Einstein to visit Riverside and participate in the honorary ceremony.

After three months in southern California, the Einsteins returned to their home in Germany. The next two winters they returned again to Pasadena where the Nobel Prize winner studied and worked at Caltech. Albert Einstein continued to generate vast attention wherever he appeared and the couple received hundreds of invitations to social and academic affairs including banquets, dinner parties, guest appearances and ceremonial fetes. He held the world's attention for 40 years and thousands of words have been written praising his legendary genius. Ironically, there was little coverage or disclosure of that embarrassing day when the grumpy old macaw Joseph pinched the finger of the most famous man in the world.

Chapter 30

PRINCE AND PRINCESS KAYA
1934

On August 31, 1934, Japan's Prince Tsunerori Kaya and his wife, Princess Toshiko Kaya, arrived in Riverside to attend a luncheon in their honor hosted by Mission Inn owner Frank Miller. The Prince was Emperor Hirohito's first cousin and the imperial couple had just concluded an extensive tour of the United States. Their motorcade was escorted from Los Angeles by the California Highway Patrol to the western entrance of Riverside where it stopped briefly at the Buena Vista Bridge. A crowd of more than 200 fellow countrymen and local officials, carrying both Japanese and American flags, enthusiastically cheered the royal couple with traditional "banzai" greetings. Princess Kaya graciously accepted a large bouquet of red roses and waved in appreciation to the colorful, kimono-clad children as the entourage proceeded on to the Mission Inn.

Upon their arrival at the Inn, the honored guests received a warm welcome from Frank Miller and officers of Riverside's Japanese Association. Following cordial introductions and greetings, the imperial couple was ushered into the Presidential Suite to meet members of the Frank Miller family. The Master of the Inn was wearing his distinguished Japanese decoration, the Fourth Order of Merit, Order of the Rising Sun that he received in March 1929. This medal was a unique award bestowed by Emperor Hirohito upon his 1928 accession to the throne. It was considered the highest honor granted by Japan and rarely given to citizens of other nations. The Emperor had acknowledged Frank Miller for his many contributions toward world peace and goodwill among nations.

The Prince and Princess were departing for Japan the following day and although pressed for time, they accepted Frank Miller's luncheon invitation, their only unofficial visit granted during their tour. Consequently, their visit to the Mission Inn was considered an informal affair although a number of prominent officials accompanied the royal couple from Los Angeles. Included in the party were several high-ranking Japanese military officers, representatives of the Japanese embassy in

Washington, D. C., officials from the State Department and Princess Kaya's lady-in-waiting.

Guests gathered in the Presidential Suite where they were served a refreshing fruit punch after their long two-hour drive from Los Angeles and, on this last day of August, a chance to cool off was most welcome. Frank Miller then escorted the Prince and Princess and members of their party to the first floor where they entered the St. Francis Atrio. The open patio was decorated with potted plants and large flags representing Japan and the United States waved from the balcony. Two tables arranged for 24 guests were covered with the Mission Inn's finest linen and silver and as the party entered the Atrio, an organ played the national anthems of both countries. While there was no evidence of the instrument, music was piped from the Inn's Music Room, some distance away, by an employee's hand signals to the organist.

Prince and Princess Kaya were seated at the head of the main table next to their host, Frank Miller and his wife Marion. Other distinguished guests included Mr. and Mrs. Harry Chandler of the *Los Angeles Times* and Dr. and Mrs. R. B. Von KleinSmid President of the University of Southern California. While the gathering enjoyed their luncheon in the outdoor atmosphere of the Atrio, security guards were posted on the balconies above. They were assigned to keep spectators out of sight to ensure the privacy of the guests eating lunch. Members of the Japanese royal family were never to be looked down upon and by tradition were to be looked up to as an act of high esteem. Accordingly, no one was allowed on the overhead balconies except an official photographer who recorded the occasion. Throughout the luncheon, a program of soft background music was relayed from the Music Room and the Mission Inn carillon chimed a traditional song.

Following lunch, Frank Miller escorted his guests into the adjacent St. Francis Chapel, completed in 1932. It was dedicated as an International Shrine for Aviators and commemorated St. Francis, patron saint of birds and, when men took to the air, of birdmen. One exterior wall was designated the Flier's Wall where famous aviators were invited to place their autographed wings and at this time there were nine inscribed wings. Within the beautiful chapel was an ornate golden altar and on opposite walls six beautiful Tiffany windows of mosaic glass. The visitors were taken into the Galeria, next to the chapel, where they viewed paintings and antique furniture. Frank Miller proudly lead the royal couple to the nearby Oriental Art Gallery where the Miller family art collection included many Chinese and Japanese works of art acquired during their 1925 visit to the Orient.

When the tour concluded, Prince and Princess Kaya and their entourage boarded waiting cars and formed a caravan led by police who controlled traffic. A parade of cars proceeded to Mount Rubidoux and stopped near the Peace Tower. The Peace Tower, dedicated to Frank Miller for his efforts to gain understanding and world peace upon his return from the Orient in 1925, was an ideal location for this special event. The occasion was to honor Shunzo Kido, a little-known Japanese man, and Prince Kaya unveiled a bronze tablet imbedded in the Peace Tower. Japanese and American flags draped the plaque that read:

"During the equestrian games of the tenth Olympiad, Lieutenant Colonel Shunzo turned aside from the prize to save his horse. He heard the low voice of Mercy, not the loud acclaim of Glory. Erected by the Riverside Humane Society. Unveiled in the presence of H.J.H. Prince Tsunerori Kaya August 31, 1934" The plaque was decorated with a design of cherry blossoms and an ancient axiom in Japanese characters. Translated it read, "Mercy is the chief attribute of a warrior."

The caravan proceeded to the summit of the mountain and the esteemed guests observed the panoramic view of surrounding areas. Citrus groves covered the hillsides and green trees of every description spread to the edge of town. Before the royal couple departed for Los Angeles, they paid tribute to their host Frank Miller and city officials for their hospitality and warm friendship. And in return, everyone wanted the Imperial Highnesses to remember their brief but historic visit to Riverside. They were presented a leather-bound book containing 25 scenic pictures of Riverside taken by well-known local photographers Avery E. Field and E. N. Fairchild. The Japanese community expressed its appreciation to Frank Miller for his prolonged interest and respect and his hospitality to Prince and Princess Kaya.

As early as 1906, the Japanese were welcome residents in Riverside. Many settled in the community and found employment or managed their own businesses. To celebrate the 56th birthday of Japan's Emperor Matsu Hito an assortment of people gathered in the Loring Opera House. Crossed flags of America and Japan were displayed over the entrance of the theater and within were additional flags and oriental lanterns. This congenial gathering subsequently became an annual event in observance of the Emperor's birthday and featured a family picnic or other organized activity.

On November 1, 1917, Frank Miller invited more than 60 local Japanese residents to a special banquet at the Mission Inn. In addition to the celebration of the Emperor's birthday, the community wanted to thank the Riverside Japanese Association for their generous subscriptions to purchase United States Liberty Bonds in the amount of $5,000 to assist the war effort. American and Japanese soldiers were fighting side by side and a fraternal spirit existed among allied nations. There were many speakers expressing appreciation delivered in both English and Japanese. For this auspicious occasion, the Mission Inn dining room was decorated with banners, flowers and huge Japanese flags draped across banquet tables. Large bouquets of colorful chrysanthemums were displayed on each table in recognition of Japan's national flower. A large portrait of the Emperor surrounded in bright flowers and crossed flags of America and Japan was prominently displayed at the head table. Local dignitaries expressed their appreciation to the Japanese people for their love of beauty, their deep respect for the aged and their love of children.

One speaker discussed Riverside's Harada case, then making national news. The case was the first anti-Japanese lawsuit filed in California under the Alien Land Law of 1913. Because he was a Japanese citizen and could not legally own California real estate, Harada recorded the deed to his Riverside home in the names of his American born children. The property involved was a modest six-room home at 3356 Lemon Street and the deed was contested by the State as unconstitutional. Eventually Harada won his case in the U.S. Supreme Court and the Alien Land Law was repealed and the matter became a precedent for others to follow.

Frank Miller died in 1935, but the Japanese continued to honor him for his efforts to promote international friendship between the United States and Japan. A delegation of Japanese dignitaries from the House of Representatives of the Imperial Japanese Diet visited Riverside in 1936 and made a pilgrimage to his grave in Evergreen Cemetery. They held a simple ceremony in his honor and invited local countrymen to attend. Throughout the years other groups of Japanese citizens including students and teachers came to Riverside to see the Mission Inn and Frank Miller's Peace Tower.

Many years after World War II in 1969, Shunzo Kido came to Riverside for the first time, accompanied by Lois Castle. George Parish, manager of the Mission Inn, escorted the guests to Mount Rubidoux and the Peace Tower where the plaque dedicated to Kido in 1934 was imbedded. He recalled the 1932 Olympic competition that he was about to win when his horse refused to jump the last hurdle. Rather than force and injure his horse, he gave up the contest and presented his saddle to a nearby equestrian named Lois Castle.

Shunzo Kido finally read and touched the bronze plaque presented by Riverside's Humane Society and dedicated and acknowledged by Imperial Highnesses Prince and Princess Kaya.

Six months after Frank Miller invited Prince and Princess Kaya to a luncheon at the Mission Inn, he extended an invitation to descendents of a famous writer, Harriet Beecher Stowe. The Beecher family reunion was organized when a renowned lecturer was scheduled to give a talk entitled *Saints, Sinners and Beechers.*

Chapter 31

THE BEECHER FAMILY
1935

When Harriet Beecher Stowe died in 1891, she had never passed through the doors of the Mission Inn. Thirty-nine years later however Frank Miller invited her descendants to be his guests and to attend a lecture delivered by her grandson Lyman Beecher Stowe. On March 24, 1935, Beecher family members and in-laws arrived to attend the unusual reunion inspired by the presence of the eminent New York lecturer whose program was entitled *Saints, Sinners and Beechers*. He was scheduled to appear at Riverside's First Congregational Church of which Frank Miller was a member.

When the invited guests arrived they assembled in the lobby to socialize and renew family ties. After sharing memories, Frank Miller escorted the party across the street to the Congregational Church where their celebrated relative would recall some accomplishments and dubious conduct of family members. Fifty-five-year-old Lyman Beecher Stowe began by explaining the Beecher family background since the audience included church members as well as relatives.

He said his great-grandfather, the Reverend Lyman Beecher, was the patriarch of the clan, a powerful, hellfire preacher who fathered 11 children. The Reverend's most illustrious offspring included his grandmother Harriet Beecher Stowe, Reverend Henry Ward Beecher, Catharine Beecher and Isabella Hooker, all endowed with distinctive talents. The family freely expressed their conflicting religious and literary opinions publicly and fought for women's rights. Lyman Stowe then discussed his grandmother's rise to fame and the support she received from her family.

Harriet Beecher Stowe had once lived in Cincinnati, Ohio, where she observed southern slaves fording the river to reach free land. The line between freedom and slavery was the Ohio River, visible from her home, where she witnessed many failed attempts to reach freedom. Her husband, Calvin, a seminary professor, and her siblings encouraged her to write about the anti-religious and moral aspects of slavery.

In 1852, her book *Uncle Tom's Cabin* was published and it became a classic on human injustices. Her story became world famous reflecting the good and evil among humans. More than seven million copies were sold during a period when few people could read. As Frank Miller listened intently to Lyman Stowe, he recalled one of his fondest childhood memories when his mother had read the story aloud to the family gathered near her chair. The fictional events produced strong emotions throughout the nation and were said by some to have triggered the Civil War. When Mrs. Stowe first met President Abraham Lincoln, he greeted her with respect but remarked, "So this is the little woman who made the big war."

Harriet Beecher Stowe had lost four children and as a result, doted on her remaining twin girls and son, Charlie. Charlie Stowe married Susie Monroe and his mother bought the couple a home in Hartford, Connecticut. He followed the Beecher tradition in the ministry and fathered two children, Susie and Lyman. "I'm proud to say he was my father," said the speaker who graduated from Harvard in 1904 and entered the publishing business where he was member of the editorial staff for Doubleday. He and his father co-authored a biographical book in 1911 entitled, *Harriet Beecher Stowe, The Story of Her Life.* Their research subsequently stimulated his interest in the historic Beecher family. Later research was used in his 1934 book entitled *Saints, Sinners and Beechers.* He recalled that this venture exposed family secrets and eccentricities attributed to some members of the non-conforming Beecher family. With a smile, Lyman Beecher related some questionable escapades of his family members.

Reverend Henry Ward Beecher, his uncle, gained an illustrious and notorious reputation as an eloquent preacher and the inspirational leader of the prestigious, old Plymouth Church in fashionable Brooklyn, New York. In spite of his sweeping fame, scandal engulfed the Reverend because of a romantic liaison with a married woman. Undaunted by the Reverend's immoral conduct, his devout followers remained loyal to the controversial, charismatic character. Riverside's Reverend Horace Porter, former minister of the First Congregational Church and once mayor of the town, was proud to have served as Reverend Beecher's assistant pastor at the Plymouth Church.

Catharine Beecher became well known for teaching women the science of domestic economics, believing that women should be educated and trained in the necessities of domestic life within the home. Her sister Isabella took an opposite stand and crusaded for the women's rights movement and encouraged females to work outside the home. In his concluding remarks, Lyman Stowe pointed out that members of his unorthodox family had unwittingly contributed varied opinions to the culture and history of the American scene.

The large audience then enjoyed a hymn written by Harriet Beecher Stowe entitled *Still, Still With Thee*. There were nine in the audience who had heard Henry Ward Beecher preach in Brooklyn and three who had known Lyman Stowe's grandmother. The Beecher name was known throughout the nation because family members often contested conventional standards of culture and religion.

Beecher relatives gathered in the Mission Inn's Presidential Suite the following day to visit and assist Lyman Stowe in his quest for family history. He had been accumulating data and ancestral charts for some time and had successfully contacted over 300 possible relatives across the nation. After much genealogical discussion, the group was escorted into the Music Room for a festive reunion luncheon.

The guest of honor was Charlotte Perkins Gilman of Pasadena, great granddaughter of the patriarch Reverend Lyman Beecher, and she was seated at the head of the table. The famous authoress and lecturer had a national reputation as a radical feminist and enjoyed a long, notable career. As a popular, renowned lecturer, she often stated, "I had plenty to say and the Beecher facility for saying it." She told the luncheon guests of her terrible bouts of depression as a young woman and how she visited friends in Pasadena to seek help. She saw a noted nerve specialist who simply diagnosed her condition as "Beecher" and would have nothing more to do with her. Sometime later, she left her husband and small child and moved west to Pasadena. As a single woman in southern California, she became actively involved in women's rights and devoted her time and energy to the movement. Many viewed her as peculiar to leave her family to devote her life to such unconventional causes. She was considered even more eccentric following her feeble attempts at acting in local amateur productions. To add to Charlotte Perkins already bizarre reputation, she married her cousin, George Houghton Gilman. In spite of her impetuous lifestyle, she became a well-known writer with a large following.

The informal atmosphere of the reunion luncheon prompted guests to share memories and Reverend Francis Ellis, pastor of Riverside's First Congregational Church, had some words for the Beecher family. He quoted from an early sermon of Henry Ward Beecher whereby he urged those in power to always do-good work and have the courage to follow their beliefs. A member of the family added that their ancestor's book, *Uncle Tom's Cabin* was still being printed in the 1930s by several different publishers and was in demand by students and libraries. In Germany the Nazi regime had banned the book declaring it did not fit into their racial ideals.

Next Alice Miller Richardson greeted the group and expressed Frank Miller's regrets that he could not join the family reunion because of illness. Mrs. Richardson was eager to share her Beecher family experience that had taken place 50 years earlier in the original Glenwood Hotel.

In 1881, Thomas K. Beecher, youngest son of the patriarch Reverend Lyman Beecher, registered at the Glenwood Hotel. Known as Thomas K. he was a preacher in Elmira, New York, where the most famous citizen in town was Samuel Clemens, also known as Mark Twain. In 1870, Thomas K. was scandalized for drinking beer and playing cards, then considered an immoral practice and not acceptable for a man of the cloth. Nevertheless, he performed the marriage ceremony for Samuel Clemens and Olivia Langdon and they attended his church regularly. Thomas Beecher had a large congregation and his parishioners allowed him to live his life as he wished.

When the Reverend visited the Glenwood, the city of Riverside had a population of 500 industrious people. Although the population was limited, there were a number of substantial churches including Baptist, Methodist, Presbyterian, Episcopal and Congregational. Mrs. Richardson recalled that the variety of churches impressed the Reverend Beecher.

At the time, 1881, Alice Miller Richardson managed the Glenwood Hotel for her brother Frank. Because of Riverside's growth and prosperity, Frank Miller decided to enlarge the original 12-room adobe house to a more pretentious two-story frame structure. He obtained a building permit for $10,212, to expand the building with the addition of two wings and the contract was awarded to Woodward & Brown. After the foundation had been laid, construction came to a halt for lack of lumber. While undergoing remodeling, the hotel remained in operation with as little discomfort to guests as possible. Reverend Thomas K. Beecher registered just as a supply of lumber was being delivered and the crew returned to work. Mrs. Richardson described how the distinguished guest eagerly assisted the construction workers and how he seemed to enjoy manual labor. He extended his visit several extra days and she praised his industrious and solicitous manner. Furthermore, she wished to express her appreciation to his distant relatives and to inform them that she never forgot his kind act of friendship and cooperation. It was an appropriate conclusion to a grand family reunion.

As members of the Beecher family left the Mission Inn, there were some descendants who may have wondered in which specific category they might fit - Saint or Sinner?

Some years later, a young man passed through the doors of the Mission Inn and decades later the American public was to ask if he had been a Saint or Sinner. In 1940, a little known private citizen named John F. Kennedy visited the Inn.

Chapter 32
JOHN FITZGERALD KENNEDY
1917-1963

In December 1940, John Kennedy traveled from Palo Alto to Riverside to attend the annual Institute of World Affairs conference held in the Mission Inn. The week long sessions involved daily round table discussions and nightly lectures delivered by eminent guest speakers. The Music Room filled each evening with an attentive audience comprised of various generations assimilating scholarly suggestions as to how best solve world problems.

When 23-year-old Kennedy arrived in Riverside, he found the Mission Inn a busy place filled with notable diplomats and college professors. From December 9 to the 14, the Institute's agenda consisted of proposed solutions regarding international conditions then creating a serious crisis in Europe. The first evening, Dr. Eliot G. Mears, Stanford professor of international trade, narrated the program. Stanford University was well-represented and encouraged educators and students alike to participate in the Riverside conference. This campus enthusiasm may have sparked John Kennedy's intellectual curiosity. After graduating from Harvard, he was attending the Stanford Business School searching for a future career. Stanford President Dr. Ray Lyman Wilbur was a former Riversider who sanctioned the Institute's exchange of ideas and publicized the upcoming programs taking place in his hometown.

After Dr. Rufus Von KleinSmid, president of the University of Southern California, was introduced, he greeted the delegates assembled in the Music Room. He had served as Chancellor of the Institute since its first meeting and his name was synonymous with the organization. He aroused the audience's attention when he said, "There will be the wildest divergence of opinion and frankest statements of disagreement at our conference. Scholars will pit their judgement against scholars but each will be afforded a most eager hearing." Morning sessions began at 8:00 a.m. followed by round table discussions until late afternoon and concluding with a summary symposium.

This challenging, intellectual atmosphere greeted John Kennedy when he arrived at the Mission Inn. He served as a rapporteur, or mediator, for several round table discussions under the supervision of Dr. Eleanor Dennison of Stanford University. His quest for knowledge and his leadership qualities enabled him to conduct stimulating dialogue among the groups of participants. At the time of his Riverside visit he was still seeking a career with a leaning toward teaching history or political science. His older brother Joe was being groomed for a political career and he wished to enter a different field. The two brothers had attended Choate School and Harvard and developed a normal sibling rivalry.

In 1937, their father, Joseph P. Kennedy, was appointed United States Ambassador to the Court of St. James in England. His fame, fortune and power had been derived from the fields of finance and commerce. When the Kennedy family moved to London, Joe and John were students at Harvard but frequently flew to England to visit their family. By design, members of the Kennedy family never traveled on the same flight. During the summer months Joe and John represented their father and met with foreign dignitaries to gather information relative to that country's latest war conditions. The young men socialized with prominent European leaders and high-ranking diplomats in England, France and Spain.

During John Kennedy's last year at Harvard he wrote his senior thesis based on his personal observations and experiences. His dissertation was entitled *Why England Slept*, an analysis of Great Britain's failure to rearm in the face of the Nazi threat. As a result of this timely project and his academic standing he graduated "magna cum laude." In 1940, the thesis was published in book form and received excellent reviews. Time magazine called it "startling timely, a terrific record of wishful thinking about peace when peace was impossible."

In the course of an interview with a local reporter concerning his book Kennedy replied, "Yes, my book has been unusually successful. It was published in this country in August and in England last October. It's in its fifth edition and has been on the *New York Tribune's* best seller list since publication." At the age of 23, John F. Kennedy was already making news in Riverside and across the nation.

Thus, when John Kennedy attended the 1940 Institute of World Affairs he was no doubt better informed of existing European war conditions than most of the distinguished lecturers participating in the conference. Because of his many trips to England, he could relate the courage and fortitude of its citizens in the face of impending disaster. But the primary emphasis of the Riverside conference was on the growing unrest in the South Pacific and the tense relations among Asian nations. One featured speaker was Dr. David Crawford, president of the University of Hawaii, who strongly expressed his opinions of Hawaii's uncertain future.

"It is inevitable that conflict will rise between this country and Japan before long and at the present time feverish defense preparations are being made in the Islands."

Another professor declared, "Peace is the most precious thing in the world but it cannot be had for nothing. We must go forth aggressively to fight for peace and the philosophies which sustain it."

Before the conclusion of the conference, there had been numerous discussions and opinions focussed on various methods that might be used in dealing with aggressive nations. Although there were no definitive conclusions, the conference was considered a success and plans were made to return the following December. After John Kennedy's brief involvement in the 1940 conference, he left for Palm Beach, Florida, to join his family for the Christmas holidays.

His parents, Joseph and Rose Kennedy, had acquired a seaside, Spanish style mansion in Florida during the 1930s depression. The $10,000 house became the family's winter headquarters where tennis courts, swimming pool and golf privileges could entertain the large family. It became a Kennedy tradition to spend the Christmas holidays in Florida, but the 1940 gathering was to be the last reunion involving the entire family. In the spring of 1941, Joe joined the Naval Aviation Cadet Program and John volunteered for the Army but failed his physical examination because of a bad back. He was determined however to join some branch of the armed services and commenced a strenuous exercise program to strengthen his back muscles. Ultimately, he joined the navy, was commissioned an ensign and served with distinction in the South Pacific.

After the war, and the death of his older brother Joe, John Kennedy's inclination for politics surfaced. In the 1950s, he served as a United States senator and later set his sights on the highest office in the nation. In Riverside, devoted Democrats organized a Kennedy Club and opened an office in the Mission Inn where volunteers worked the phones, passed out political brochures and held fund raising rallies. They were delighted when their candidate John F. Kennedy visited Riverside in November of 1959.

In October he planned a four-day tour of California, starting in Oakland and ending in Los Angeles. He scheduled a brief appearance in Riverside to attend a political rally for D. S. Saund, Congressman for Riverside and Imperial counties. On Sunday, November 1, Senator Kennedy arrived at the Riverside Municipal Airport after a half-hour flight from Burbank. A welcoming committee of Riverside officials and Democratic leaders escorted him to the Mission Inn for a public reception in the Spanish Art Gallery. He spoke briefly about the issues of the cold war and said, "If we permit the Soviet Union to assume the robes of progress, then it is quite obvious that smaller nations will turn away from us and turn to the Soviet Union. The problem of our time is the United States' relationship to the Communist world and to the rest of the non-Communist world." After 20 minutes, he left the Mission Inn to attend a barbecue rally at Arnold Heights School near March Air Force Base.

His schedule was accelerated to allow him time to visit Congressman Saund at the March Field Hospital where Saund was recuperating from physical exhaustion. Saund's wife accompanied Kennedy and when they arrived at the barbecue, they were warmly received and Kennedy flashed his broad smile in appreciation. He was so busy answering questions and greeting supporters that he was unable to participate in the barbecue before his quick departure for another rally at Disneyland. His Riverside appearance had lasted less than two hours.

Two months later, in January 1960, Senator Kennedy formally entered the race for his party's presidential nomination. During the Democratic convention in Los Angeles, John F. Kennedy was selected as its candidate and a strategic plan was formulated to aid his campaign. His younger brother, Robert Kennedy, became his campaign manager with other members of the family serving on his election committee. Both candidates, John Kennedy and Republican Richard Nixon, covered more than 60,000 miles on the presidential campaign resulting in the most arduous on record. They criss-crossed the nation time after time visiting four or five states in a day.

Teddy Kennedy came to Riverside to support the election of his brother. He held a 15-minute rally in front of the Riverside County

Courthouse on Main Street and delivered a short speech standing on the seat of a convertible. Before departing for another rally, he evidently had lunch in the Mission Inn where he signed his name on a book of matches. Notable people were frequently asked for their autographs on menus, cocktail napkins and other memorabilia.

Needless to say, John F. Kennedy became the 35th President of the United States. The 43-year-old dealt with the great coalitions of East and West, each capable of awesome destruction. Despite volumes of information about the life and times of John F. Kennedy, little has been recorded of his participation in Riverside's Institute of World Affairs. The frank discussions and free expressions of opinions of learned scholars and educators may have influenced his beliefs and thoughts in obtaining world peace. The Institute of World Affairs was the forerunner of the present World Affairs Council that frequently meets in the Mission Inn.

His younger brother Robert passed through the doors of the Mission Inn 18 years after John Kennedy's 1959 quick campaign appearance. Robert Kennedy was also striving to obtain the highest office in the United States.

Chapter 33

JUDY GARLAND
1922-1969

Actress Judy Garland visited the Mission Inn in 1942 with her musician husband David Rose. They were married July 27, 1941 in a surprise weekend elopement to Las Vegas accompanied by her mother and stepfather. When the news was made public, many were unhappy about the union including Louis B. Mayer, head of Metro-Golden-Mayer Studio. His disapproval of the marriage was so intense that he refused her time for a honeymoon and the following day resumed filming of the movie *Babes On Broadway*. As a result, it was some time later that the couple decided to visit the desert, stopping at the Mission Inn en route.

Judy Garland had been associated with David Rose since February 1940 when he accompanied her on the piano and arranged her musical scores. They continued as a team for several months making motion pictures and recordings. At the time Rose was married to the comedy-variety star Martha Raye who appeared in pictures and benefit performances. Martha Raye and David Rose were later divorced but studio officials and Judy Garland's family remained opposed to the budding romance. Rose was ten years her senior and considerably more sophisticated than the teenager.

David Rose was born in England in 1910 and moved to Chicago with his family when only four years old. He attended public schools and later studied music, a talent he faithfully pursued. After completing his education he was hired as a pianist for a Chicago radio station and in 1938 he joined the Ted Fiorito orchestra and became proficient in the latest popular music. These early experiences inspired him to become a musical director and he later played for radio, movies, recording studios and television. As a Hollywood musical director, he accompanied the talented Judy Garland, the teenager who spent her life in show business.

When Judy Garland was two years old, she appeared with her sisters Susie and Jimmie in amateur theatrical productions in their hometown of Grand Rapids, Minnesota. Their parents, Ethel and Frank Gumm, billed their three daughters as the Gumm Sisters and little Frances later become known as Judy Garland. While mother Ethel played the piano and father Frank managed a small theater, the girls sang and danced for charity shows and local social events. Frances made every attempt to keep up with her older sisters to please her parents and gain their approval.

In order to expand professional opportunities, the family moved to southern California and settled in Lancaster. By September 1928, the Gumm girls were working in Los Angeles part-time with a professional children's group. Little Frances Gumm had a strong voice with notable intensity that could be heard over and above an entire orchestra. In addition she danced with smooth, flowing movements and quickly learned difficult dance routines. Frances always tried to please the audience and worked diligently to perfect her song and dance routines.

In 1933, the Gumm family moved to Los Angeles where Frances and her sisters were enrolled in Lawlor's Hollywood Professional School. She befriended a fellow student named Mickey Rooney, who was to become a lifelong friend. After two years of acting school, the Gumm sisters signed a contract with MGM and joined a vaudeville tour in the east. In Chicago they were a last minute replacement in a performance that included George Jessel. He was impressed with the act especially the booming voice of young Frances. At his suggestion, the Gumm sisters changed their name to Garland, taken from the *New York World Telegram* drama critic, Robert Garland. Judy selected her new first name in 1935, when she was 13.

In addition to being an excellent dancer, Judy had perfect pitch and a photographic memory and once she read a script, she knew each part and every cue. With all her diversified abilities, however, MGM did not utilize her varied talents for several years. In the meantime she sang with various orchestras, recorded popular songs and gradually obtained small movie roles. In 1937 she performed with Mickey Rooney for the first time in the movie *Thoroughbreds Don't Cry*. The teenagers worked well together and subsequently toured the United States promoting their film. They followed rules set by Louis B. Mayer whose influence was stronger than that of a parent. Actors under contract were considered studio property and were given strict guidelines of behavior. However, when Rooney and Garland traveled to promote their *Andy Hardy* series Judy's mother Ethel chaperoned the two. The young actors performed slapstick routines throughout the country and high school crowds soon became devoted fans.

Louis Mayer purchased the film rights to the book *The Wizard of Oz* for $75,000 and hired the first of five directors used to make the musical fantasy. Because of her youthful appearance and past experience in such roles, Judy Garland was cast as Dorothy. Although in her teens at the time, she managed to remain believable in her role as a young girl throughout two years of filming. She had an abundance of energy and during that period she attended school, made personal appearances and recorded the latest hit songs. In spite of her busy schedule and active lifestyle, however, she had a tendency to gain weight and in order to control the problem her family and studio officials arranged for her to take Benzedrine. At the time the addictive nature of the drug was not well known and Garland soon found that the stimulant made sleep difficult, if not impossible. To counteract the effects of Benzedrine she took sleeping pills and the combination of the two resulted in frequent bouts of depression and emotional instability that were of deep concern to her co-workers. Later in life Judy Garland was to blame her mother for her problems and criticized MGM for the mismanagement of her early career.

The Wizard of Oz opened in New York City in 1939 and soon became one of the biggest box-office attractions in movie history. It remains a great classic to this day and has been translated into virtually every language. In accordance with the provisions of her contract with MGM, 17-year-old Judy Garland spent the next several months on a promotional tour throughout the country publicizing the new film. At the time the teenager became romantically involved with bandleader Artie Shaw, threatening the studio's efforts to project her wholesome image. In spite of the disapproval of her affair with an older man, she continued to meet Shaw with the aid of her sister, Jimmie, and close friend, actor Jackie Cooper. This romantic interlude went on until she learned of the sudden and unexpected elopement of Artie Shaw and actress Lana Turner. The betrayal devastated Judy and added to her drug dependency. Following this bitter disappointment she became completely immersed in her work. She sang on the radio and made dozens of best selling records including her recording of *Over The Rainbow*. It remained on top of the charts for months.

David Rose supervised her recording sessions and they began dating in 1940. In the spring of 1941, her last *Andy Hardy* picture premiered and a few months later she began filming *Babes On Broadway*. Judy

Garland was aware that the studio executives would be displeased with her marriage to David Rose, an older divorced man, and opted to quietly elope to Las Vegas. With no time off she finished the film and when it was released on Broadway World War II had been declared.

During the war, the Mission Inn housed thousands of service men and their families and seldom was there an empty room to be found. Riverside became the hub of numerous military bases with nearby March Field (later March Air Force Base), Camp Haan adjacent to March, and Camp Anza southwest of town. The navy established a base in Norco and the army took over the San Bernardino Airbase (later Norton Air Force Base). Consequently, thousands of service men on leave gravitated to Riverside and the Mission Inn became a place to meet. The Lea Lea Room, a cocktail lounge and nightclub with a relaxed South Seas atmosphere, became a favorite spot among G.I.s where they could drink, dance and romance local girls. During this unsettled period when the nation was preparing for an all-out war, Judy Garland and David Rose visited the Mission Inn where they dined in the Spanish Patio. This may have been one of the few times the busy couple could relax and enjoy each other.

Soon both performers joined Hollywood troupes that went from base to base to entertain thousands of service men. Judy Garland shared the stage with stars Lucille Ball, Fred Astaire, Harpo Marx, Mickey Rooney and Kay Kyser. At each military base they participated in a two-hour parade, a lengthy press conference and an evening show. In addition to appearing at army camps, Judy Garland was one of the brightest stars in the movie industry and continued to appear in one picture after another. She often worked on two movies at the same time. In 1943 she began the picture *Meet Me In St. Louis* directed by Vincente Minnelli, who later became her second husband. In January 1945, she played a prospective mail order bride in the musical *The Harvey Girls*. Her peers in the motion picture industry admired Judy Garland's stamina and many talents, including Cary Grant, a good friend, who faithfully collected her sheet music and recordings.

In the summer of 1969, 47-year-old Judy Garland died in her London cottage from an accidental overdose of sleeping pills. Throughout the world grieving fans mourned her untimely death and fondly remembered the talented actress as a happy young girl named Dorothy in the 1939 classic, *The Wizard Of Oz*. A mourner commented,

"No one had the personality and talent to hold an audience as she did."

Twenty-eight years after her death, Judy Garland was remembered in her hometown of Grand Rapids, Minnesota, where a Judy Jubilee Festival and new children's museum debuted. The jubilee marked the 75th anniversary of the star's birth. Family members discussed highlights in Judy Garland's life and collectors exhibited Garland memorabilia. The museum displayed the carriage used in the movie, a yellow brick road and hundreds of red poppies.

The Mission Inn returned to a quiet, peaceful atmosphere after World War II and, in 1947, another cherished movie star known as America's Sweetheart passed through the doors of the hotel. Mary Pickford came as a private citizen to accept the presidency of the Women's International Association of Aeronautics.

Chapter 34

MARY PICKFORD
1892-1979

Petite actress Mary Pickford walked through the doors of the Mission Inn on a bright spring day in 1947. Dressed in a smartly tailored suit and perky small hat, she was familiar with the hotel and went directly to the Music Room. She and her handsome husband, Buddy Rogers, had visited the hotel throughout the years and had been guests on special occasions.

The retired movie star descended the steps into the sunken Music Room where she was greeted warmly by her good friend Mrs. Ulysses Grant McQueen. Mrs. McQueen, acting as hostess, welcomed those who had come to attend the 18th annual meeting of the Women's International Association of Aeronautics. Those in attendance were mostly veteran fliers who gathered annually to renew friendships and keep abreast of the latest aviation news. The presence of Mary Pickford, however, had little to do with flying even though she was to be inducted as the new president of the organization

Elizabeth McQueen, more often known as Queenie, was the founder and honorary president of the group. She presided over the opening ceremonies and welcomed the members to the Mission Inn. At the time she was a permanent resident at the hotel and her overwhelming feeling of hospitality extended to the membership of the WIAA. The exuberant hostess graciously introduced special guests including Lady Chaytor of London whose presence made the affair truly international. Mary Pickford took over the meeting as the new president and congratulated the organization on its 18th birthday. She read several congratulatory telegrams from well known fliers such as Eddie Rickenbacker, perhaps the most famous aviator of World War I, and aviatrix Ruth Law Oliver of San Francisco.

Although Mary Pickford and Mrs. McQueen were not pilots, they both supported the advancement of aviation and strongly endorsed the work of the WIAA. Mary Pickford had her first flight with Glenn Martin in 1915 and soon discovered the excitement of flying. In later years, she became a regular air-line passenger and frequently traveled by air throughout the United States and Europe. When President Pickford addressed the distinguished members of the WIAA she praised the ladies for their dedication and achievements in the field of aviation. The audience, no doubt, was pleased to have the support and endorsement of the former movie star, once considered the most famous actress of her time. In addition to her prestigious name, the new president was well known for her astute business sense and driving ambition.

The remarkable evolution of Toronto-born Gladys Marie Smith into the famous actress known as Mary Pickford began in New York during the early days of the motion picture industry. While still a teenager, she changed her name to Mary and adopted her grandmother's name of Pickford. She appeared on the Broadway stage under the direction of David Belasco and considered this the highlight of her career. In 1908, the young girl made her first motion picture directed by David Wark Griffith. He encouraged her use of child-like movements and expressions to reflect a wholesome, innocent little girl. Barely five feet tall, Mary appeared much younger than her years and her helpless girl image created a vast, dedicated audience. She earned $5 a day in melodramatic heroine roles and the half-hour "flicks" were shown in nickelodeons across the nation.

During the winter of 1910, D.W. Griffith and his movie company left New York to seek more moderate year round weather in southern California. The ambitious actress appeared in six to eight films a year with the talented director who emphasized her child-like image by featuring long spiral curls, frilly dresses and no make-up. Movie sets were made larger so that the actress would appear even smaller than normal. These silent films were sold and distributed to theaters throughout the country including Riverside and in 1915, *Miss Nell* starring Mary Pickford played at the Regent Theater on Main Street.

Mary Pickford earned sizeable salaries from her acting and received 50 percent of the net profit from each picture. Between her lucrative acting contracts and her shrewd investments she accumulated great wealth. In 1916, when she was 24, the silent screen actress earned more than the President of the United States. Inventor Thomas Edison labeled her "America's Sweetheart" because of her simple charm and the public's preoccupation with her private life.

In 1920, the radiant Mary Pickford married handsome movie star

Douglas Fairbanks and the public labeled the couple the "King and Queen of America." The flamboyant Hollywood stars moved into a 22-room Tudor style mansion, appropriately christened *Pickfair*. Located in Beverly Hills on a hill in Benedict Canyon, the house became a social center for the elite of Hollywood. Each lavish party at *Pickfair* was attentively described in detail in both newspapers and movie magazines. Thousands of curious admirers followed the lives of Mary Pickford and Douglas Fairbanks.

The ambitious couple joined Charlie Chaplin and D.W. Griffith in organizing the United Artists Corporation. The company grew into the leading movie studio in Hollywood and had the ability to both produce and distribute their own films. Mary Pickford gained a sharp business sense as a partner in the corporation and became a shrewd businesswoman with a strong will and determined attitude. In addition to producing and distributing moving pictures, Pickford and Fairbanks continued to appear in silent films.

In 1927, the 35 year-old actress starred in *My Best Girl,* her last silent picture, with actor Charles Rogers as her leading man. The young man, nicknamed Buddy, had an easy-going personality and was readily accepted by the cast and crew. During production he became deeply attracted to the leading lady, an affection that resulted in his marriage to Mary Pickford ten years later.

After her final silent film, the youthful appearing actress cut her long golden, corkscrew curls and renewed her image to that of a mature young woman. In spite of her great popularity, her fans could not accept this transformation and soon centered their attention on promising new actresses. With the advent of sound, Pickford quickly learned that her high pitched voice was not acceptable and after more than 200 successful silent films and four talkies, she retired in 1932. A younger generation of moviegoers emerged with new idols and favorite heroes, ending Mary Pickford's illustrious career as an actress.

In 1934, Douglas Fairbanks was named correspondent in a divorce suit and the "King and Queen of America" separated. The life and times of Pickford and Fairbanks made headline news for months and finally the actress filed for divorce in 1936. She retained the deed to *Pickfair* where she lived an additional 43 years until her death. She took refuge with friends and admirer Buddy Rogers who offered companionship during the long divorce proceedings. The former actress had been deprived of an admiring audience with the advent of talking pictures and then lost the great love of her life through divorce.

Mary Pickford and Buddy Rogers married in June 1937 and moved into *Pickfair*. During this time he was the leader of a touring dance band and played one night stands, often away from home on the road. Mary Pickford occasionally traveled with her husband to avoid the loneliness at *Pickfair*. She became involved in charity work and offered her name, time and money to aid philanthropic endeavors. Her friend Queenie, Mrs. McQueen, encouraged her to become a member of her favorite organization of female pilots and to serve as president of the WIAA. A year later, Pickford invited board members to a reception tea held at *Pickfair* and she continued to endorse the work and educational commitments of the group long after her term of office expired.

Some years later, the petite actress became a semi-alcoholic and remained in seclusion at *Pickfair*. She was a disturbed recluse for the last 13 years of her life, loved and cared for by her devoted husband Buddy Rogers. "America's Sweetheart" died peacefully in 1979 and her death received worldwide news coverage, as did the details of her estate. Her musician husband inherited *Pickfair*, a "cottage" in Palm Springs and income from a trust fund. The bulk of her estate was endowed to the Mary Pickford Foundation for the benefit of religious, scientific, and educational institutions.

Buddy Rogers sold *Pickfair* in 1980 and built a more grandiose home on a portion of the property. The following year he married Beverly Ricono, a Beverly Hills real estate agent and long-time friend. The couple spent a great deal of time in the desert where he pursued his passion for golf and played to a nine handicap.

Later in 1981, a shiny black Rolls Royce stopped at the entrance to the Mission Inn where Buddy Rogers and his wife Beverly emerged. They entered the hotel and strolled through the lobby inquiring about the Inn and its future. Sue Johnson, a member of the Mission Inn Foundation, was in the lobby at the time and offered to be of assistance. Although she did not immediately recognize Rogers and his companion, she graciously escorted the couple through the public rooms. The interested visitors were told that Riverside's Redevelopment Agency had owned the Mission Inn since 1976 and had leased the property to the Mission Inn

Foundation for five years. The Inn had been in jeopardy of being demolished and the City had become involved in order to renovate and restore the building to its historic grandeur.

As Mrs. Johnson guided Barbara and Buddy Rogers through the hotel, he began to reminisce about "his good times spent at the Inn" and recalled that he and Mary had been guests there during the 1920s and 1930s. He thanked her for her interest and the couple proceeded to the Presidential Lounge only to discover it was closed until late afternoon. In lieu of a cocktail, Buddy Rogers remembered once enjoying ice cream at the corner drugstore. He then learned that Banks Drug Store had been closed for years and the visitors returned to their Rolls Royce and left Riverside.

Changing times had affected the allure of the Mission Inn just as they had diminished Mary Pickford's cinematic illusions. When astute businessman Benjamin Swig purchased the antiquated Mission Inn in 1957, he also became disillusioned when he attempted to update and modernize the hotel.

Chapter 35

BENJAMIN HARRISON SWIG
1893-1980

Bold headlines appeared in Riverside newspapers on May 18, 1956 announcing the optimistic news "Mission Inn Here Sold to S. F.'s Fairmont Hotel." The major stockholders in the Frank A. Miller Corporation signed documents transferring title to the Fairmont Hotel Company managed by Benjamin Swig. The property consisted of the Mission Inn building, its two-and-one-half acre site, a parking lot, an employee housing structure on Sixth Street, a service station on Main Street, the Fairmount Park Golf Course and several unimproved lots at the base of Mount Rubidoux. Although no actual price was publicly acknowledged, it was rumored to have been a two million-dollar transaction.

Ben Swig's successful operation of the historic San Francisco hotel, and other grand hostelries, had earned him an enviable reputation for providing quality service and pleasant accommodations. After acquiring the Mission Inn, he expressed his pleasure in working with the business community of Riverside and announced his intentions to revitalize the aging hotel. He planned to renovate and refurbish the 250-room hotel in order to increase the diminishing tourist trade. Although many local citizens were eager to see the downtown landmark thriving once again, many were apprehensive about an outsider taking over the city's most prestigious asset. In spite of this underlying resentment, Ben Swig arrived in town with the best credentials and a reputation as a distinguished hotel operator and generous philanthropist.

Born into a large Lithuanian immigrant family in Boston, young Swig went to work at an early age to help support his family. He preferred to be known as Ben and friends and family used that version of his name. On December 24, 1916, he married Mae Aronovitz and they subsequently had three children, Melvin, Betty and Richard. Swig entered the finance and commerce fields and invested in real estate. He and his family became active in the Jewish community and served as volunteers in various religious groups. Through the years, Swig met with success and gradually accumulated a small fortune only to lose everything in the

1929 stock market crash

Starting a new career, he specialized in developing commercial property and skillfully put together intricate real estate transactions for national businesses and chain stores. Because of his successful business ventures, Ben Swing became well known with offices in Boston and New York. In 1944, he purchased the St. Francis Hotel, a popular San Francisco hotel with a high occupancy rate during World War II. San Francisco, a debarkation point for the armed services, suffered an acute housing shortage and hotels remained fully occupied. In 1945, Swig purchased San Francisco's historic Fairmont Hotel on Nob Hill and his family moved west. His other real estate investments included the Russ Building and Mills Building in downtown San Francisco. In 1956, his real estate company purchased the Arrowhead Springs Hotel in San Bernardino County but this proved to be a poor investment and it was sold three years later.

The Fairmont Hotel was considered the jewel of Ben Swig's real estate empire. Its existence was partly due to James G. Fair, a partner in the rich Nevada Comstock silver mines. As one of the Bonanza Kings, he gained great wealth but remained a controversial character all his life. After six years as a U.S. Senator, and surviving a sensational divorce, he died leaving a huge estate that was in litigation for years. Eventually James Fair's Nob Hill home was inherited by his daughters, Mrs. William K. Vanderbilt and Mrs. Herman Oelrich. The ladies aspired to build the grandest hotel in the west on the Nob Hill site and plans were drawn and construction began. No expense was spared and the Fair sisters spent over five million dollars building the elaborate hotel. Just as the magnificent, grand opening was to take place in 1906, the San Francisco earthquake and fire destroyed the building on April 18. Undaunted by this catastrophic event, the determined sisters rebuilt the luxurious hotel with the help of a little known local architect named Julia Morgan. The new Fairmont opened one year later to the day on April 18, 1907. Thirty years later, the Swig family moved into the Fairmont and it was their home for many years.

In June 1956, Ben Swig arrived at the Mission Inn full of enthusiasm with the intention of making it attractive and comfortable without sacrificing its historic appeal. His plans called for no basic changes to the structure and he hired Barbara Dorn of San Francisco to supervise the interior decorating. Dusty curtains and faded carpets were replaced and the 1920s light fixtures were up-dated to meet Riverside's building codes. A new color scheme was added and old furnishings were replaced in an effort to modernize the antiquated interior.

At a luncheon held in the Spanish Art Gallery for city officials, Ben Swig suggested that being an outsider in town might prove beneficial because he could see things that could be changed. He expressed his interest in Riverside but added that it needed more industry, more downtown parking and he questioned the city's future, noting many closed stores and deserted buildings. He proposed a mall of some type along Main Street that might bring families to downtown, especially if there were children's play areas. Ben Swig pledged $50,000 to the city of Riverside to start a feasible project that would "dramatize Riverside."

For a year and a half, major work was underway renovating the Mission Inn. During this period, the Institute of World Affairs moved their annual meetings to the Huntington Hotel in Pasadena. The gift shop sold some surplus items and, in July 1957, a public auction further reduced the number of antiques and artifacts. Although Ben Swig retained many important works of art and various collections accumulated by the Miller family, numerous citizens viewed the auction as a "rape" of the Mission Inn.

On December 13, 1957, Mr. Swig's son Richard and hotel manager David Danolds greeted 400 guests at an open house cocktail party to unveil the refurbished hotel. Guest rooms had been painted and furnished with a combination of antique and modern furniture. One hundred and twenty-five bathrooms had new plumbing and most of the hotel was air-conditioned. One major change was the relocation of the St. Cecilia Chapel from a small alcove in the Music Room to a condensed chapel facing the St. Francis Atrio. In addition, the former Cantina, a small restaurant west of the lobby, became the Squire Arms Bar and Grill and featured a medieval atmosphere. The cardinal red carpeting and matching swag drapes complimented the heavy ornate shields and coats of arms displayed on the walls. Leather upholstered booths and small tables could accommodate 75 patrons. In addition Swig established two cocktail lounges and the Lea Lea Room was restored, featuring nightly dancing.

After investing one million dollars in repairs and remodeling, management reported an additional one million-dollar loss in unrealized rental revenues. Swig anticipated, however, that the Mission Inn would soon improve and predicted that business would be better than ever. He held majority interests in six other hotels including the Fairmont Hotels in San Francisco, Chicago, Dallas, New Orleans, Boston and New York.

The Riverside Downtown Mall opened in 1966, financed with a special district bond backed by surrounding property owners. Four blocks on Main Street became a pedestrian walk with areas of grass, landscaped trees and children's playground. Although it was thought that the mall would attract shoppers downtown, it fell short of expectations. The pedestrian mall extended a full block adjacent to the Mission Inn, however, business continued to be slow and the hotel experienced low occupancy. Changing trends forced stores to leave the area and to relocate in neighborhood malls.

In July 1967, the Goldco-M II Company took over the operation of the Inn and assumed a two million dollar first mortgage on the property held by Ben Swig. He continued to take part in Riverside activities and to oversee his investment in the Mission Inn. When asked to serve on the board of trustees of the new Riverside University, he did not hesitate and traveled often to Riverside for scheduled meetings. The school, originally a local business college, subsequently reorganized as a school of education where many students enrolled under the G.I. Bill of Rights. In 1968, Ben Swig received a Doctor of Commerce Science degree from the university at graduation ceremonies held in the Music Room of the Mission Inn. It was later discovered that the school had not been accredited by the Western College Association and did not qualify under the veterans benefits program.

When Goldco-M II declared bankruptcy in 1969, the doors of the Mission Inn were padlocked for the first time in its history. The Inn reopened later under Ben Swig's ownership and bankruptcy trustee management. A private student-housing firm, known as Scope, leased one hundred rooms and filled them with students from the University of California at Riverside. There were three occupants to a room and the students took refuge in the lobby to read and socialize. By the end of the Scope contract, the Inn's occupancy rate had dropped 24 percent and lost $300,000 in a year. In June 1971, the Mission Inn closed for the second time.

Ben Swig, who owned 57 percent of the Mission Inn stock, offered to sell the hotel to the City of Riverside for $750,000. The City Council seriously considered the offer but could not find a way to raise the money. Swig told the officials, "I want to see it remain as a city cultural asset. I'm willing to take a big loss and to carry the remaining debt five, ten, or fifteen years or more. I want to help." The council appreciated Mr. Swig's efforts to preserve the hotel and his desire to cooperate with the city and its people.

The mortgage listed in the Inn bankruptcy papers amounted to two million dollars and Swig stated that the total indebtedness to his group of investors came to well over that specified amount. Ben Swig, and his silent partners Charles Benenson of New York and Donald Walters of Riverside, Connecticut, had kept the ailing Mission Inn operating through the hectic years of the 1960s, in spite of personal losses.

From 1970 to 1992 the Mission Inn experienced a series of owners and a hectic existence. In 1985, the Carley Capital Group of Madison, Wisconsin, purchased the Inn and began a two-year restoration. The project went over budget and in 1988 the property was transferred to Chemical Bank of New York, the Carley Group's principal creditors. Local businessman Duane R. Roberts of the Historic Mission Inn Company purchased the refurbished Mission Inn in December 1992 and thus began a new era for Riverside.

Chapter 36

ROBERT FRANCIS KENNEDY
1925-1968

United States Senator from New York Robert Kennedy was a Democratic presidential candidate when he arrived in Riverside for a brief reception on May 29, 1968. After leaving a successful rally in San Bernardino, the Kennedy motorcade exited the freeway at Seventh Street and traveled to the corner of Park Avenue where several hundred people eagerly awaited his arrival. When he finally appeared the enthusiastic crowd came to life with cheers, reaching to touch him and hopefully to get his autograph or other souvenir. Robert Kennedy had become a political icon, idolized by all generations and ethic groups.

After addressing 400 admirers on the street corner, his motorcade traveled to the Mission Inn where a block of rooms had been reserved for Ethel and Robert Kennedy and members of his campaign. The Kennedy entourage had been on the road for weeks and had just experienced a serious political loss in Oregon. The campaigners were in need of a rest and shower before the Riverside rally that evening.

Earlier that day, the Kennedys had arrived in southern California mindful of a substantial change in the political scene. Senator Eugene McCarthy had just won the Oregon primary and the fight for delegates became even more critical in the final week of the campaign. While McCarthy toured California's Central Valley, Kennedy traveled throughout southern California. An upbeat atmosphere prevailed, nevertheless, as the Kennedy motorcade traveled through the business district of Los Angeles. Huge crowds forced the closure of major streets as traffic came to a halt for the caravan of cars. Blaring loudspeakers attracted additional spectators along the parade route and a smiling Robert Kennedy sat on the back seat of an open convertible visible to the mass of humanity lining the streets. Confetti rained from the windows high above his head and, whenever his car stopped, men tried to shake his hand and women reached out to touch him. Senator Kennedy would frequently stand and shout, "I'm going to be the next President of the United States. I need your help." Everyone screamed and cheered and although the police admonished pedestrians to remain on the sidewalks, their warnings were ignored.

After the rousing parade through Los Angeles, the revitalized candidate delivered several political speeches before his local volunteers and loyal followers. Ethel and Robert Kennedy attended a luncheon at the Beverly Hilton Hotel in Beverly Hills seeking financial support for the Democratic convention. That afternoon, as the temperature reached 100 degrees, the Kennedy motorcade headed for Fontana, San Bernardino and Riverside. Upon their arrival at Pioneer Park in San Bernardino, a crowd of 6,000 greeted Robert Kennedy with loud applause even though they had waited an hour beyond his scheduled arrival. Kennedy called for racial understanding and equal educational opportunities for all Americans. Placards reading, "Kennedy A Man of Ideas" and "Sock It To 'Em Bobby," popped in the air and were followed by more cheers and applause. He promised the Pioneer Park supporters he would not be satisfied until "the Vietnam War was over and American soldiers brought home." He advocated tax concessions to stimulate housing development and was gratified to note the favorable reactions of the enthusiastic crowd.

Riverside had planned a simple reception for the Kennedys on May 29 to be held at the Municipal Auditorium with the Senator scheduled to appear briefly around 8 p.m. Early that evening, three thousand people filled the auditorium eager to show their support and to have an opportunity to be in the presence of a Kennedy. A public address system was installed on Seventh Street to relay his message to the large overflow of devoted admirers. Entertainment was provided prior to the Senator's arrival by a rock band, a campaign film and local singers. The audience grew restless as the minutes ticked away and by 9 p.m. their candidate had not yet appeared.

Robert Kennedy left the Mission Inn about nine o'clock and walked the one block to the auditorium, accompanied by his companion-bodyguard, Rafer Johnson, the Olympic decathlon champion. Ethel Kennedy opted to remain at the hotel and rest while her husband made his appearance at the "brief, simple reception." When Kennedy and Johnson entered the auditorium after nine o'clock, the weary crowd came to life with screams, shrieks and whistles. Dozens of campaign posters shot in the air as their guest of honor fought his way to the stage. Because of the surging crowd, husky volunteers hoisted the Senator onto the stage where he could be seen by all. He eventually calmed the audience and gained their rapt attention. Dramatically, he removed his jacket, rolled up his shirtsleeves and cheerfully addressed his gregarious supporters.

He repeated his familiar phrase, "I need your help, I think we can do better," and the building exploded with applause. After a few remarks, the restless crowd moved closer to the stage to be near their idol and one woman leaped on the stage and quickly embraced him. Young girls screamed to get his attention while others shouted, "I touched him. I touched him." When several handshakes became too physical, his campaign workers held him steady and asked the crowd for restraint.

During his speech, the Senator touched on the major themes of his campaign and although the audience had heard it before, they rallied with enthusiasm on every point. He had previously stated that "under no circumstances would he accept the nomination for vice-president" and stressed the need for strong supporters to ensure his nomination. He noted the poor needed jobs, not welfare, and that the federal government should be more responsive to the needs of all people. He advocated an end to the war in Vietnam through a negotiated settlement and a gradual withdrawal with government assisted reforms. Kennedy declared he was campaigning on a platform of political reality, the politics of optimism, and loud applause and shouts of "RFK for president" immediately followed his statements.

While downtown streets were closed for the Robert Kennedy reception, opponents were arriving for a local fund-raising party. Supporters of the other Democratic presidential candidate, Eugene McCarthy, gathered in the Dunes Restaurant in the Plaza Mall to hear a rock group called the Music Express. The McCarthy party ran from nine until midnight and conveniently overlapped Robert Kennedy's appearance in the Municipal Auditorium.

At the conclusion of Kennedy's address, he moved across the stage shaking hands as he headed for a side door exit and proceeded down a delivery ramp to a waiting car, replacing his jacket as he hurried along. After settling into a convertible waiting to take him to the Mission Inn, he sat on the back seat as the crowd came rushing towards him. Smiles and good cheer did not quell the swarm of advancing people who pulled at his coat and knocked him off balance. Rafer Johnson helped him gain his composure and held him around the waist to protect him from toppling over. Police had previously blocked off streets around the auditorium and the restless crowd milled around downtown long after Kennedy had left the area. Young fans ran around the streets yelling "Bobby! Bobby!" and no one wanted the warm Memorial Day eve to end.

When Robert Kennedy returned to the Mission Inn, he had trouble remembering which room he had been assigned. A bellman noticed his query and came to his rescue by directing him to the correct room. The New York Senator had started campaigning in March and after months of traveling it became difficult to tell one hotel room from another. All the candidates were beginning to feel the effects of the strenuous routine of campaigning, especially in the final week before the convention.

An hour after Robert Kennedy found his room, his motorcade assembled in front of the hotel and his entourage left for Los Angeles to spend the night. The following week was busy with personal appearances and on June 5, the candidate was in Los Angeles again. Eight days after his Riverside reception, Robert Kennedy was killed by an assassin's bullet at the conclusion of a rally in the Los Angeles Biltmore Hotel. People were shocked to hear the news of his death as it spread throughout the world. Members of the Kennedy family received heartfelt condolences and sympathy including messages from many Riverside citizens.

Memorial services were held throughout Riverside County for Robert F. Kennedy and it was a time for individual and collective prayers for his family and for the nation. Many Riverside churches held services on Saturday and Sunday, June 8 and 9, and special masses were held in Catholic churches. The Council of Churches of Riverside and San Bernardino issued a list of Kennedy services for the convenience of all congregations. Flags flew at half-staff and scheduled events in Riverside were cancelled. Gestures of respect extended to the closure of some supermarkets for a short period as Riverside joined the nation to pay tribute to a most recent visitor.

Local citizens, who had seen and heard the Senator the week before, would never forget the experience. Dr. Francis Carney, professor at the University of California, Riverside and chairman of the Riverside Kennedy campaign, had sometimes feared for the Senator's safety and felt he might be a target in his public appearances. Local volunteers requested the American Legion to provide the proper procedure for draping the flag and use of black bunting.

A formal funeral service was held at St. Patrick's Cathedral in New

York City as citizens across the nation paused in silence to observe the moment. Thousands of families watched the chain of events on television and radio stations played solemn music. Ethel Kennedy assured the public that the thousands of letters and cards sent to the family would be acknowledged. A special 21-car train transported the Senator, his family and close friends to Washington, D. C. where he was laid to rest in Arlington National Cemetery. A brief and simple ceremony took place at 11 p.m. as a band played *America The Beautiful*.

Robert Kennedy's short stay in Riverside is still remembered by many people who recall that hot night in Riverside's Municipal Auditorium where he removed his coat and was very much at ease in the midst of chaos.

Later that year, another audience filled the Municipal Auditorium to hear a violin concert featuring Jack Benny. The popular comedian appeared in a fund-raising performance to benefit the Riverside Symphony Orchestra.

Albert Einstein and wife Elsa visited the Mission Inn in January 1931.

The Alhambra Suite occupied by Grand Duke Alexander in 1930.

The tall, dignified Grand Duke (center) planted a palm tree in Low Park March 29, 1930, and expressed hope world peace and love would flourish as well as the tree.

Heber J. Grant, seventh president of the Church of Jesus Christ of Latter Day Saints stayed at the Mission Inn.

On Easter Sunday, April 21, 1930, Heber Grant dedicated the Mormon Church at the northeast corner of Locust and Third Streets.
RLHRC Photo

Will Rogers in vaudeville.

*Will Rogers and Janet Gaynor
in "The State Fair."*

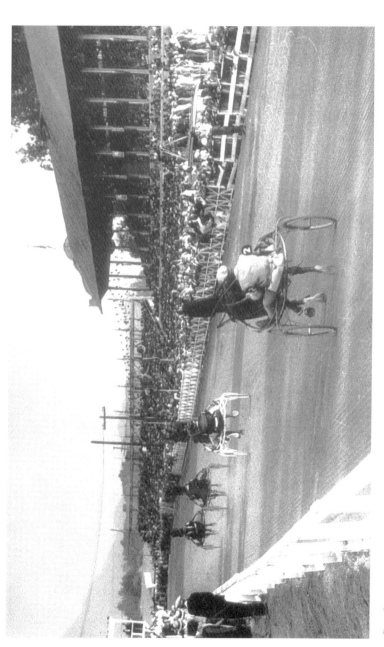

The Southern California Fair Grounds near Fairmount Park was a location frequently used by motion picture companies.

Reception for Prince and Princess Kaya of Japan when they arrived in Riverside.

Frank Miller held a private luncheon in the Atrio to honor Prince and Princess Kaya.

In a tailored suit and perky hat, actress Mary Pickford posed in front of the Flier's Wall in 1947.

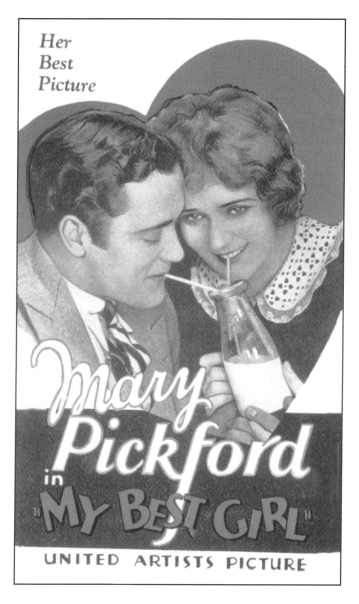

Her
Best
Picture

Mary
Pickford
in
"**MY BEST GIRL**"

UNITED ARTISTS PICTURE

Mary Pickford and Buddy Rogers first appeared together in "My Best Girl."

Actress Judy Garland and husband David Rose enjoyed au fresco dining in the Spanish Patio.

Jack Benny and James Guthrie rehearsing for a benefit concert in Riverside's Municipal Auditorium.

Twenty-eight year-old Cary Grant (left) was an aspiring movie star when he visited Palm Springs in 1932.

Jack Lemmon and Walter Matthau in 1981 with the Aguilar boys, Joseph, Jaysen and Johnathan.

As the Mission Inn wedding coordinator, Jane Margison supervised more than 3000 ceremonies.

Chapter 37

JACK BENNY
1894-1974

After comedian Jack Benny retired from telecasting his weekly show, he began a new career performing in musical concerts for fundraising benefits. These concerts took place throughout the United States and provided him the opportunity to play the violin with some of the world's finest musicians. His performances raised more than five million dollars and assisted numerous struggling, insolvent symphony orchestras. In 1968 three organizations were selected for his personal appearance of which the Riverside Symphony Orchestra was one.

His decision to perform in Riverside may have been influenced by an earlier acquaintance with its musical director, James Guthrie. Their friendship dated back to World War 11 when performers donated their talents to entertain servicemen at nearby military bases. Jack Benny did his routine at the El Capitan Theater in Hollywood where he first met James Guthrie. Guthrie was the substitute orchestra leader at the theater and soon discovered the difficulty in providing music for spontaneous, unrehearsed acts. Stars would appear unannounced, go on stage and begin their routine as he attempted to provide background music. However, when Jack Benny appeared on stage and played the violin in a comedy skit, Guthrie expertly directed the orchestra to accompany him. Guthrie later recalled conducting more than 20 shows featuring the humorist-violinist.

On Thursday evening, December 5, 1968, Jack Benny and James Guthrie were reunited on the stage of the Riverside Municipal Auditorium after more than 25 years. The rehearsal session went smoothly as Benny went through his comic routine entertaining the musicians and building maintenance crew. He played his $5,000 Stradivarius violin, skillfully pausing between notes with his patented blank stare. He told the orchestra that the people he worked with were told to keep a straight face "but the rest of you can laugh whenever you feel like it." He quickly added, "You'd better laugh or otherwise I'm in trouble with the people out front." Benny added, "I don't play lousy on purpose, that's just the way I play."

Despite his frequent interruptions, he took his music seriously and produced proficient symphonic renditions. Many musicians suspected his desire to be an accomplished violinist although Benny confessed that comedy became more important than his music. After two hours of rehearsals, the comedian was satisfied with the program and praised members of the orchestra for their valuable cooperation. He added that he was pleased to have the opportunity to play with such talented professionals and expressed his gratitude.

The Riverside Symphony Orchestra set a goal of $25,000 from ticket sales from Jack Benny's concert. Proceeds were to pay a backlog of debts and to establish a firm foundation for future operations. Organizers of the Benny benefit realized that in order to fill the 1800-seat auditorium the bulk of the tickets would have to be priced at no more than five dollars. However a limited number of $50 tickets, entitled purchasers to attend an after-show champagne reception at the home of Dr. Ivan Hinderaker, Chancellor of the University of California, Riverside. Tickets were available at the Harris' Department Store and Cheney's Music Store and a promotional brochure noted that they were tax deductible and approved by "tightwad" Jack Benny.

A capacity audience filled the auditorium for the Saturday night concert that was declared a huge success. Everyone enjoyed Jack Benny's humorous anecdotes and clean jokes, usually centered on himself. The penny-pinching actor let it be known he was being paid to play his fiddle and added; "no one would ever see that nickel again." His slow deliberate delivery and excellent timing had been well developed during his many years performing on radio, television and stage. Throughout the evening, James Guthrie provided excellent musical accompaniment and his spirited, athletic style amused the audience. Members of the orchestra and the comedian thoroughly enjoyed producing serious music and later Benny commented that the evening was one of the most pleasant of his 11 years performing such concerts.

Following the show the guest of honor was driven to the Chancellor's home in an antique classic 1922 Chevy. Guests were eager to meet the man from Waukegan, Illinois, who had achieved super-star status in the entertainment field. The Hinderaker's had redecorated the Watkins Drive mansion adding their personal touch with a yellow carpet and cheery birch paneled walls. Although this was the chancellor's residence, more than 3,000 visitors a year used the facilities for UCR meetings and dinners. The champagne reception to meet Jack Benny was a huge success as he warmly greeted his fans who would long remember the evening. The Riverside Symphony Orchestra raised $17,000 from the event and after expenses and debts, the organization realized $13,000. Riverside music enthusiasts were most grateful for the opportunity to enjoy good music, clean humor and the opportunity to provide for the orchestra's future.

Jack Benny attracted large audiences wherever he appeared but it took many years to achieve star status. He began show business as a teenager after joining a musical vaudeville act in which he played the fiddle. Later, he developed his own skit and called it "Fiddleology and Fun." In the late 1920s, radio became popular and in 1932 he was a guest on the Ed Sullivan Show, his first radio appearance. Later he signed a contract for his own radio show that featured skits centered on himself or members of the cast. The American public approved of his style, especially the references to his frugality. In 1940, the highest accolade radio could confer went to Jack Benny when the Crossley Research Organization named his show first in a list of the ten best radio programs of the year. Other shows included the popular family radio programs of Fibber McGee & Molly, Charlie McCarthy, Bob Hope and Major Bowles.

In 1950, the United States radio and television editors were polled to determine the public's favorite shows and performers of the year. Jack Benny was voted Radio Man of the Year and the most popular comedy show was Jack Benny's program. The survey for television viewers concluded the Man of the Year was Sid Caesar and the most watched comedy show was awarded to Milton Berle. After many years on radio, Benny appeared on television and soon starred in his own weekly show. He earned eight Emmy Awards for his flawless timing and comedy style.

Whenever Jack Benny revisited Riverside he was always welcomed as an esteemed local benefactor for having donated his time and talents. In 1969, he was awarded an honorary Doctorate of Music from the Riverside University in recognition of his contributions to the Riverside Symphony Orchestra. The two-year-old university had evolved from the former Riverside Business College, a long-established local vocational school. Riverside University president George Holgate invited Jack Benny, Ben Swig and Mayor Joseph Alioto of San Francisco to attend the school's second graduation exercise and to receive special honorary degrees.

On Saturday, June 28, 1969, prior to graduation exercises, the Riverside University's alumni association hosted its first annual luncheon in the California Room of the Mission Inn where the board of directors and newly elected alumni officers discussed a proposed program of activities for the coming year. In the evening the second commencement service was held in the Music Room with San Francisco Mayor Joseph Alioto guest speaker.

Alioto urged the 118 graduating students to take swift action against "hard core campus militants who want confrontation and disruption for disruption's sake." He advocated campus and state officials to prosecute those who engage in violence and to work for reforms. He encouraged the students to use their newly acquired knowledge to help America's poor and to bring about a better understanding between races. His short speech was not entirely confrontational and was peppered with bits of humor as he wished them success and fulfillment in their new endeavors. Mayor Alioto received an honorary degree of Doctor of Commercial Sciences presented by university president George J. Holgate and trustee Ben Swig. Comedian Jack Benny, dressed in a black cap and gown, was awarded an honorary Doctor of Music degree for his extensive contributions to the musical world. In accepting the award, he said it was one of the great thrills of his life and, never out of character, added, "Apparently no one here has ever heard me play the violin." It was obvious the 75-year-old entertainer was pleased to receive a Doctorate of Music and he received a standing ovation.

Later when the graduates and celebrities were socializing, Mayor Alioto admitted he had played the violin in his youth but had kept his questionable talents a secret. Jack Benny then confessed he didn't play the violin as well as Jascha Heifetz and recalled his vaudeville days when he played jazz rather than classical music. The delightful evening came to an end and it was destined to be the last commencement of the Riverside University.

The Riverside University opened in 1968 and grew rapidly with a diverse curriculum, a new and challenging faculty and an impressive board of trustees. Students first met in the classrooms of old Lincoln Grammar School on Lime Street and later in various other locations.

Many students required government loans and it was finally disclosed that the Western College Association had not accredited the school. Government loans could not be obtained for non-accredited colleges. Bookkeeping discrepancies and the lack of qualifications of some faculty members came to light and the school eventually went into bankruptcy.

Jack Benny's benefit concert in Riverside resulted in a firm financial foundation for the continued performances of the symphony orchestra. The furor over the defunct Riverside University did not diminish his pleasure in obtaining a Doctor of Music degree, especially when it was awarded in the grand Music Room of the historic Mission Inn.

Another well-known entertainer passed through the doors of the Mission Inn in 1977 when Cary Grant suddenly decided to revisit the hotel after attending Frank Sinatra's mother's funeral in Cathedral City.

Chapter 38

CARY GRANT
1904-1986

On a cold afternoon in January 1977, a tall handsome man and his attractive female companion passed through the doors of the Mission Inn. Movie idol Cary Grant stopped at the Inn while returning from Palm Springs to Los Angeles after attending the funeral of Frank Sinatra's mother. When the debonair movie star entered the lobby unannounced he was easily recognizable and heads turned to stare at the popular star. Grant asked the desk clerk if he could be given a brief 15-minute tour to locate the room he once occupied in the 1930s while making a film.

Employee Robyn Stanger courteously accommodated the couple and escorted them through the lobby pointing out objects of interest while relating the hotel's history and uncertain future. She guided them to the Court of the Birds and explained that the Inn had been remodeled several times since the 1930s including the addition of the swimming pool in the courtyard. Grant thought he recognized an ornate bay window on the second floor and concluded that it was the room where he had stayed while making the film. He could not recall its name because he had made seven or eight movies a year. The actor was so intrigued that he requested to see more of the hotel and the 15-minute tour stretched into an hour and a-half.

As they strolled through the building, he expressed his approval and fascination with the various architectural styles. He compared the hotel to the William Randolph Hearst Castle in San Simeon where he had been a frequent houseguest. When it was time to leave Grant gave Stanger a one hundred-dollar bill for her personalized tour and hoped that the hotel would be restored and preserved. He recalled early childhood memories of ancient buildings in England that had suffered from neglect and eventual demolition.

Cary Grant was born Archibald Alec Leach to a relatively poor family in Bristol, England, the child of frustrated entertainers. His parents encouraged their teenage son to join the Pender Troupe, a family of energetic acrobats. He specialized in stilt walking and comedy pantomime and when unemployed, worked odd jobs in music halls and theaters to learn the techniques of stage productions.

In 1918, he joined the Pender family on tour through England and Europe and after two years they were booked into the New York Hippodrome. It was Leach's first visit to the United States and although he wanted to remain, he continued his routine with the Penders in England.

Later, seven performers in the troupe, including Leach, signed a contract to tour the United States with their final performance in Los Angeles. After criss-crossing the country to the west coast they visited Hollywood before returning to New York where they decided to remain. Archie Leach had matured into a handsome young man with dark hair and a well-proportioned physique. Although he had little stage experience, he appeared in musical plays and audiences soon discovered that the young man had little musical talent.

By 1927, he had modified his cockney accent and refined his mannerisms in an effort to emulate his idol actor Fredric March. Leach subsequently developed his own easy style that pleased the American public and featured a British accent and gentlemanly manners.

At the age of 26, the struggling actor moved to Hollywood where his successful screen test at Paramount Pictures resulted in a bit part as second romantic lead. His contract called for a name change to ensure a more recognizable identity. First known as Cary Lockwood, his surname was later changed to Grant by studio officials. As a poised, articulate actor, studios promoted his manly image by pairing him with famous actresses and budding starlets when attending well-publicized social events. Hollywood gossip columnists kept his name in print as long as he lived.

With his photogenic good looks and easy-going manner, Grant was cast in a variety of films ranging from *Gunga Din* to *Madame Butterfly*. He appeared with Mae West in *She Done Him Wrong* and was the recipient of West's most famous line, "Why don't you come up n' see me sometime?" In 1937, he starred in a *Topper* picture with Constance Bennett and portrayed the sophisticated gentleman that ultimately led to his box-office popularity. He became a huge success and frequently worked concurrently on two films, moving from one set to another with the challenging task of instantly changing characters and roles.

In 1940, he appeared in *The Philadelphia* Story starring Katharine

Hepburn and James Stewart that became a huge financial success and eventually a film classic. His salary for the picture amounted to $137,000 and was donated to the British War Relief Fund. Grant was known as a prudent person with a conservative reputation and his act of generosity was reported throughout the country greatly increasing his popularity and the picture's ratings. He played hero roles during the war years and starred in *Destination Tokyo* and later portrayed Cole Porter in *Night and Day*. Grant was nominated for Best Actor in the Academy Awards for *Penny Serenade* in 1941 and *None But The Lonely Heart* in 1944.

During his early years in Hollywood he befriended many entertainers including close friends Gracie Allen and George Burns and singers Judy Garland and Frank Sinatra. Ever the ladies man, Cary Grant married five times and had one child, Jennifer, whom he idolized. As a multimillionaire he maintained several homes but his mansion in Benedict Canyon remained his principal residence. Before his marriage to Dyan Cannon, in 1964, he purchased a house near Palm Springs.

Desert communities had become retreats for successful businessmen and movie stars with pleasant winter weather and plentiful recreational facilities. Stars built secluded gated houses and spent much of their leisure time in the desert. Whenever Cary Grant occupied his Palm Springs house, he socialized with fellow actors and his good friend Frank Sinatra.

In 1966, he became more selective in accepting roles and quietly retired without fanfare. He wanted to be remembered as a leading man after starring in 72 pictures during his 35 years in Hollywood. He was not content to be idle, however, and soon became involved in a variety of business ventures including a long association with Faberge, a cosmetic company. He frequently traveled to Europe on business where he remained popular and was treated royally.

In 1970, Cary Grant received an honorary Oscar from the Motion Picture Academy during ceremonies in the Dorothy Chandler Pavilion in Los Angeles. Film clips from several of his pictures appeared on a large screen to the pleasure of the celebrity-filled theater and when he came on stage, he received a standing ovation. His friend Frank Sinatra was the master of ceremonies and introduced the actor by commenting, "No one has brought more pleasure to more people for so many years, and nobody has done so many things as well. Cary has so much skill that he makes it all look easy." An emotional Cary Grant modestly accepted his honorary Oscar. Later when the Friar's Club held a party honoring Grant, Frank Sinatra again acted as toastmaster and Hollywood members roasted their good friend who always enjoyed a good joke and was amused by the good fellowship.

Several years later, Frank Sinatra gave a birthday party for his mother, Natalie, and, as his gift to her, he presented Cary Grant. Mrs. Sinatra adored the actor and claimed it was all she ever wanted and her exclusive gift became a friendly joke. An aging Cary Grant remained dapper as ever in his well-tailored clothing and dashing style and he continued to attract women of all ages with his full head of silver hair and tan wrinkle-free face. Wherever he appeared, ladies clamored to get a better look at the "Silver Fox" who occasionally was accompanied by bodyguards.

In January 1976, Frank Sinatra's mother was killed in an airplane accident on her way from Palm Springs to Las Vegas to attend the opening of her son's engagement at Caesar's Palace. The Lear Jet crashed into the side of Mount San Gorgonio about 25 miles from Palm Springs. A snowstorm had reduced visibility and bad weather was blamed for the crash. Funeral services in Cathedral City drew hundreds of celebrities including Cary Grant, singer Dean Martin, comedian Red Skelton, actress Ginger Rogers and Nancy and Ronald Reagan. After a Catholic Mass, 60 cars drove to the private burial services where dozens of floral arrangements were displayed. The following day, January 13 Cary Grant visited the Mission Inn and recognized Room 220 as his previous quarters during filming in Riverside.

The aging Silver Fox began a new career in 1982 and appeared in one-man shows entitled "A Conversation With Cary Grant." He took his 90-minute act around the country and filled local theaters with both new and old generations. He sat on a wooden stool in the middle of the stage and talked about his life in general and his Hollywood acting days. This was followed by a series of film clips from several of his best-known movies with comments interjected about different scenes. After the clips, he would answer questions from the audience and interact with the public in a question and answer session. Discussions centered on changing cinema techniques and public opinion and film ratings. This relaxed format drew capacity crowds and many came to participate in his informal evenings and to visit with a famous celebrity. In return, Grant enjoyed the close attention of an attentive audience and it made him feel somewhat younger than his actual age. Decades earlier, Will Rogers had used the same format on radio and although the two men were dissimilar, each appealed to the general public because of his genuine qualities and sincere charm.

Near the end of November 1989, Cary Grant was scheduled to appear in a small theater in Davenport, Iowa, but the evening performance was canceled when he became ill. The actor appeared normal during the afternoon rehearsal but his wife, Barbara Harris, noticed he needed help when leaving the stage. He was rushed to a hospital after feeling ill and died later that evening of a stroke. The 82-year-old Englishman had come a long way since balancing on a pair of stilts with a traveling acrobatic troupe.

Several years after Grant's 1977 visit to the Mission Inn another Hollywood contingent filled the hotel. MGM officials had selected Riverside as the ideal site for their future film starring Jack Lemmon and Walter Matthau.

Chapter 39

JACK LEMMON
1925

Billy Wilder, veteran director, producer and writer, chose the city of Riverside as the locale for his 54 motion picture. He had searched in Arizona, New Mexico and California to find a picturesque courthouse with an adjacent hotel before selecting the classic 1903 Riverside County Courthouse, even though it required construction of a hotel facade on a nearby office building. The ornate courthouse provided the ideal background for his MGM movie *Buddy Buddy*.

Preliminary arrangements for filming the picture took months of planning to obtain necessary city permits and to complete legal arrangements for use of private property. The biggest problem, however, was to arrange housing for several hundred people for an indefinite period of time. Leading actors Jack Lemmon and Walter Matthau were registered at the Mission Inn where many of the rooms had been converted into private apartments. A diverse group of renters occupied 128 apartments and there was little socializing with the actors because of their busy schedule.

The ten million dollar production was a story about two men registered at the fictitious Ramona Hotel in Riverside, California. The illusion of a hotel was created with a three-story, $200,000 facade spanning several business buildings across from the courthouse on Main Street. It featured arched windows, wrought iron accents and red tile overhangs with a classic neon sign identifying it as the Ramona Hotel. The temporary structure was used for exterior background scenes and interior shots took place in the lobby of the Mission Inn. Main Street merchants were compensated for use of their property and loss of business and MGM paid $9,000 for use of the Inn's lobby for three days.

The plot of *Buddy Buddy* revolved around Jack Lemmon's character who planned to commit suicide because of a broken marriage and Walter Matthau, a hit man, eager to silence a witness about to testify before a grand jury. Lemmon's character interferes with the mobster's plans and the story develops into a slapstick comedy. They chase one another, fall, slide and stumble through scene after scene without use of stand-ins.

On Wednesday February 11, 1981, Billy Wilder began filming with outdoor scenes scheduled in front of the Ramona Hotel. When the weatherman predicted rain, the crew set-up equipment in the lobby of the Mission Inn for interior shots. The Inn was still in operation and the public directed out of camera range. Minor changes were made including the enlargement of the check-in desk and a "Garage" neon sign displayed over the dining room doors. The company converted the Inn-Credible Gift Corner, operated by the Friends of the Mission Inn volunteers, to a newsstand where Lemmon appears in a scene purchasing lighter fluid to set himself afire. Actors and crew worked long days with several retakes and adjustments to lighting and sound equipment.

At the end of the first day of filming, Jack Lemmon, Walter Matthau and Billy Wilder went to a local Mexican restaurant. An MGM public relations agent had prepared a list of suitable Riverside restaurants and the three men decided on Temple del Sol on University Avenue. They arrived without reservations, unannounced, and a young waitress showed them their table. She recognized Walter Matthau only and with great fanfare, Matthau introduced his companions. Joe Aguilar, owner of the restaurant, emerged from the kitchen and warmly greeted the celebrities, followed by Mrs. Aguilar with her camera who photographed Lemmon and Matthau with their three sons. Other patrons acknowledged the celebrities and the spontaneous welcome evolved into a memorable evening.

On the following day, filming continued in the Mission Inn and the script called for the appearance of several policemen who wore authentic police uniforms with borrowed arm patches from the Riverside Police Department. At the end of the workday, several actors in uniform met in the Presidential Lounge and were reported to the Riverside Police Department for drinking while on duty. All actors were subsequently advised to immediately change costumes at the conclusion of their filming and the studio officials apologized to the police department.

When the production manager sought 150 extras for a courthouse crowd scene, Tom Greene, a popular columnist for the *Press-Enterprise* was among them. He wrote of his experiences in his daily column and on one occasion told how he waited hours to be in the mob scene only to be informed by a loud, impersonal bullhorn that he wasn't needed.

Later that afternoon, a strong Santa Ana wind collapsed the facade of the Ramona Hotel parking structure necessitating the evacuation of the area. Carpenters soon repaired the damage, needed only for the next scene. Local people watched the filming and grew attached to the hotel facade that they hoped might remain. To have a motion picture filmed locally was a treat and townspeople viewed the performances of Lemmon and Matthau whenever possible.

There were few major problems in producing *Buddy Buddy* although Wilder knew it wasn't an Oscar winning picture. He had worked previously with the two talented actors and the three men had developed a cordial working relationship that extended into their private lives. Although they had diverse backgrounds, it was Jack Lemmon's abundant nervous energy, hearty handshake and happy greeting that fans long remembered. His father had been a successful traveling salesman and his mother a Boston socialite. They provided their young son with piano lessons and soon discovered he had the ability to play music by ear. Although he claimed to be just an average student, he received a Harvard education and later pursued an acting career in New York. While seeking employment in show business, he worked as a waiter, played the piano and took parts in theater productions. After working in radio soap operas and small bit parts on television, his acting career took off after he appeared on the Kraft Music Hall television series.

His television experience resulted in a Hollywood screen test and in 1950 he signed a contract with Columbia Studios. Although studio officials thought he should change his name to one with more appeal he kept his birth name and subsequently made it famous. During his first years in Hollywood he had minor roles but the studio soon recognized his amazing versatility. He considered acting a full time job and became a work-a-holic spending long hours perfecting his skills. Directors and producers considered him a professional and production crews found him easy to work with. In addition to his compulsive work ethic, he possessed an abundance of nervous energy and everyone enjoyed his company.

Billy Wilder had previously written the script for *Some Like It Hot* starring Jack Lemmon and Tony Curtis and the humorous picture became a classic film. During its 1959 production, Lemmon and Austrian born Wilder became close friends and when Lemmon married Felicia Farr in Europe, Wilder was his best man. Wilder took the actor to his birthplace and former home in Vienna where he told of the loss of his family in the holocaust.

From 1961 to 1964, Jack Lemmon made one picture a year with the exception of the hit *Days of Wine and Roses* with Lee Remick that was two years in production. Billy Wilder produced *Irma La Douce* featuring Jack Lemmon and the successful *Odd Couple* with the team of Lemmon and Matthau. The two stars first appeared together in the 1966 movie, *The Fortune Cookie,* written, directed and produced by Billy Wilder. Lemmon was then an established Hollywood actor while Walter Matthau, although a successful Broadway actor, attracted little national recognition. The actors met for the first time on the set when Wilder introduced them and eventually a close rapport developed between the three men.

In spite of Lemmon's tremendous career, several of his films were disappointing including the dramatic films *Tribute* and *The China Syndrome.* These pictures were not well received and were unprofitable primarily because of their depressing nature. Nevertheless, he managed to escape the Hollywood turmoil by relaxing in his Beverly Hills home and pursuing his two great passions, golf and the piano. When Wilder approached him to costar with his friend Matthau in *Buddy Buddy,* he looked forward to working with his friends in a comedy. It was the fourth screen pairing of the actors.

On December 10, 1981, 19 Riverside community agencies sponsored a benefit gala in the Mission Inn before the movie was premiered at the United Artists Cinema at Tyler Mall. The coordinated efforts were under the auspices of the Riverside Volunteer Center and each agency supported the fund raising event. The cost of the champagne party was $25 and over four hundred tickets were sold. An auction of items used in the movie brought an additional $400 and with other generous donations the total amounted to over $11,000. Each agency received $260 after expenses. The official world premiere of *Buddy Buddy* had taken place the previous night in Los Angeles with a concurrent screening and party in Newport Beach.

Although the picture featured well-known comedians, it received poor reviews. Tom Greene wrote that the movie was weak, a comedy of cheap laughs and consisted of "unabashed stereotypes." He felt many scenes were not humorous and some of the bit actors appeared embarrassed in their roles. In a more positive vein he wrote, "Whatever the film's weakness, Riverside comes off marvelously. There are a lot of palm trees in the film, a nice feel of southern California. Look closely and you'll see fleecy clouds in the blue sky. Assure all the relatives back east that it's like that all the time. The inside of the Mission Inn looks wonderful. The lobby elevator gets into the movie and thank goodness they remodeled it last year. I'm happy to report Riverside looks great and critics will leap to their feet when they get a load of this place."

Jack Lemmon had not used stand-ins for his action shots in the movie and later complained of aches and pains. He told his golfing buddies that his bruises from falling and stumbling while chasing Matthau in his latest picture had definitely affected his game. It was common knowledge that his passion for golf was greater than his skill but his good nature and witty attitude made playing golf with him a memorable experience. Many Riverside people will long remember the Ramona Hotel and the two characters that were the only registered guests.

Chapter 40

STICK 'EM UP

For many years Frank Miller placed inconspicuous price tags on selected Mission Inn furnishings and art objects in addition to other gifts in his curio shop for the convenience of his guests. In spite of these conventional methods of obtaining mementos of the Inn, guests and employees frequently simply walked off with valuable items. Since hotels rely on their good reputations and respectable images, robberies and embezzlements were seldom reported and remained a private matter. Although the Mission Inn has retained the image of safety, comfort and security, there have been a few reprobates who have passed through its doors and uttered "Stick 'em up."

On February 10, 1890, a disconcerting incident occurred in the Glenwood Hotel when Robert W. Waterman, Governor of California was robbed. He was in Riverside for the opening ceremonies held in the Loring Opera House for the first agricultural fair of the Twenty-Eighth District. Although citrus fairs had been held locally since 1879, this event embraced San Bernardino County that then included the city of Riverside. Waterman was a successful San Bernardino businessman who had been elected lieutenant governor in 1886 and became governor following Governor Washington Barlett's death.

A large audience filled the Loring Opera House to hear Governor Waterman speak on the importance of the county's agriculture and the need for greater production of food crops. At the conclusion of the program, Waterman and his secretary-assistant walked to the Glenwood Hotel to spend the night where they found the Miller family in mourning. Christopher Columbus Miller, patriarch of the family, had died that morning. Waterman retired to his room exhausted from his long day.

Between two and three a.m. he awakened sensing that someone was in his room and soon discovered that he had been robbed. He aroused his assistant, who was in another room, and informed him that his valuable gold watch, a special timepiece from the California Senate, and several gold nuggets worth $65 were missing. The commotion in the hallway brought manager Frank Richardson and the three men examined the Governor's door lock. They found that a burglar had used a pair of "nippers" in the keyhole, fastened it to the end of the key and turned it to unlock the door. Later the police were notified of the robbery and it became a matter of record although the culprit was not found and the objects were never recovered.

During the ensuing years, the Mission Inn enjoyed an excellent reputation for its hospitality and security and guests often left their doors unlocked and made no effort to conceal valuable jewelry. After World War II, however, the grandeur of the Inn began to fade with changing times and a new generation of guests and employees. During the 1950s, a husband and wife were sightseeing in the Catacombs adjacent to the Music Room. As they walked along the narrow block long path, with but one entrance and exit, they failed to notice two teenaged boys following them. The couple enjoyed the historic displays and artwork exhibited on the wall alcoves until they heard "Stick 'em up" and looked into the barrel of a gun. The boys took the woman's jewelry and the man's money and exited the Catacombs. When the woman screamed, bellmen rushed to the scene as the boys reached the Ramona Court leading to the lobby. One husky bellman stood at the top of the stairs blocking their path and calmly said, "Give me the gun boys" as he held out his hand. They gave up the weapon without a struggle. Police were summoned from adjacent police headquarters, now the present municipal museum, and arrested the teenagers for armed robbery.

In the 1960s there were many petty in-house thefts including employee time cards, paintings, vases and knickknacks. On one occasion an upholstered chair that traditionally stood near the lobby entrance was taken with no clue as to its disappearance. Later, a desk clerk received an anonymous telephone call disclosing that the chair could be found at the Boy Scout Camp near the Buena Vista Bridge and the Santa Ana River. It was recovered and suffered no damage from its strange experience and there was never an explanation of its disappearance.

In 1974, a bronze plaque was pried from an exterior wall of the Mission Inn. The Native Sons of the Golden West had dedicated it to commemorate the 1940 marriage of Richard Nixon and Patricia Ryan in the Mission Inn and had placed it near the entrance in 1969 for public display. Appeals were issued for the safe return of the plaque and days passed before the police department received a phone call revealing that it could be found in a secluded area in Jurupa Hills. It was quickly recovered without damage and today it is prominently displayed in the lobby attached to an inside wall near the Presidential Lounge where the Nixons were married.

One of the most brazen attempts to acquire a Mission Inn souvenir occurred in 1974 when a two-ton truck and a forklift pulled into the hotel's driveway. It was just before dark when the driver unhooked the forklift from the truck and drove close to one of two ancient cannons facing Seventh Street. The Spanish cannons had been there for years and enjoyed by generations of schoolchildren. The truck driver placed the extended forklift arms beneath the wooden carriage of one cannon and attempted to lift it from the ground. It was too heavy, however, and the rear wheels of the forklift tilted up and didn't budge the cannon. A security guard soon arrived and discovered the unsuccessful attempt as a group of spectators gathered and peeled the masking tape from the truck door that revealed it to have been rented from a Montclair agency. Apparently the driver wanted a unique backyard decoration, but instead ended up with rental equipment expense, an attempted robbery citation and his word never to set foot in Riverside again.

In 1977, a young man entered the hotel lobby at 2:30 a.m. with an arm full of old statues and approached the night clerk offering to return two angels that he had stolen as a teenager. One was of wood and the other of plaster, both designed in Gothic style. He told the clerk he had removed them from the west wall, was soon leaving the country and wanted to clear his guilty conscience. He confessed taking the statues because the previous hotel owners "didn't take care of such beautiful things." Furthermore, he said since the hotel now belonged to the Riverside Redevelopment Agency, hence the people of Riverside, he felt compelled to return the stolen property.

During the turbulent 1980s, the Mission Inn received a great deal of adverse publicity as a result of a number of legal battles involving employees and their alleged thefts. Daily bank deposits were short or missing, bookkeeping accounts were inaccurate, and a Mission Inn clerk was accused of stealing over $50,000. Executives were charged with poor management until the financial records were finally corrected after a complete audit of the hotel's bookkeeping. Although these events were criminal acts, the sound of "Stick 'Em Up" was even more disconcerting to a group of Inn employees attending to their daily duties on a busy

Monday morning in 1980.

On February 4, 1980, two men walked into the Inn's business office located in the Ramona Court and held 11 Mission Inn employees captive. One was armed with a knife and the other with a gun. The office was busy at 9:30 on a Monday morning when department managers tallied weekend receipts. As the two men entered the outer office, a payroll clerk at a desk near the door was amused at the pair, thinking they were involved in a prank. It was immediately apparent to others however that this was a real stick up and no laughing matter. The gunman was later described as Hispanic, about five feet four inches tall, with a black moustache and wearing a baseball cap. The other subject was in his 20s with shoulder length blonde hair. They ordered their captives to keep their eyes down and to avoid visual contact.

Eight people were forced into a small room at the rear of the office and told to lie on the floor face down. A maintenance man made his untimely entrance into the office and was instructed to join the others on the floor. One of the robbers produced a brown paper bag and commanded Kim Baker, the food and beverage director, to put the stacked money on the desks into the bag. The knife wielder who was wearing sunglasses was becoming more agitated when he thought Baker wasn't moving quickly enough and screamed at the nervous group on the floor to, "Get down, get down, you, you, you." The man with the gun held it at his side and managed not to threaten the victims. When the cash, checks and credit slips were deposited in the paper bag, the pair exited from a small door at the back of the office. They passed through the kitchen to Sixth Street and disappeared. Although the captives had been instructed not to observe the intruders, Jane Margison had inconspicuously noted the suspect's features.

Jane Margison had been a faithful employee for 13 years when the bold robbery took place. After May Spiller's retirement in 1967, she had become a tour guide, taking guests through the hotel relating its architecture and history. She also coordinated and supervised over 3,000 Mission Inn weddings and witnessed a variety of ceremonies. The multitalented Margison was an asset to the hotel and filled many positions before her retirement. Ironically, while Jane Margison was a captive, face down on the floor, she received a phone call from movie star Bette Davis. When no one answered because of the tense situation, Miss Davis left a message advising that she had been married at the Mission Inn only once and to relay this information to the tour guides.

As news of the robbery traveled throughout the hotel, the German chef rushed into the crowded office with a bottle of vodka for the victims to quiet their nerves. The two armed men made off with $27,000. and were never apprehended.

In 1992 when Riverside businessman Duane Roberts purchased the Mission Inn he immediately opened the beautifully restored hotel to the public. It again offers safety, comfort and security to its guests and to numerous generations of famous and not so famous people who continue to pass through its doors.

BIBLIOGRAPHY

Allen, Frederick Lewis, *The Great Pierpont Morgan*, Harper Brothers Publishers, New York, 1949

Barry, Kathleen, *Susan B. Anthony*, New York University Press, New York, 1988

Berner, Bertha, *Mrs. Leland Stanford*, Stanford University Press, California, 1935

Caughey, John Walton, *Hubert Howe Bancroft*, University of California Press, Berkeley, 1946

Clapesattle, Helen, *The Doctors Mayo*, University of Minnesota Press, Minneopolis, 1944

Damon, Ethel M., *Sanford Ballard Dole and His Hawaii*, Hawaiian Historical Society, Palo Alto, 1957

Duncan, Eidelberg, Harris, *Masterworks of Louis Comfort Tiffany*, Harry N. Abrams Publisher, New York, 1942

Eyman, Scott, *Mary Pickford America's Sweetheart*, Donald L. Fine Inc., New York, 1996

Fricke, John, *Judy Garland*, Henry Holt & Company, New York, 1992

Gale, Zona, *Frank Miller of the Mission Inn*, Appleton-Century Company, New York, 1939

Gilbertson, Catherine, *Harriet Beecher Stowe*, Appleton-Century Company, New York, 1937

Gronowicz, Antoni, *Modjeska, Her Life and Loves*, Thomas Yoseloff, New York, 1956

Kotsilibas, Davis James, *Great Times Good Times, The Odyssey of Maurice Barrymore*, Doubleday & Company, New York, 1977

Muir, Leo J., *A Century of Mormon Activities in California*, Deseret News Press, Salt Lake City

O'Brien, P. J., *Will Rogers*, P. J. O'Brien, 1935

Olcott, Charles S., *The Life of William McKinley*, Houghton-Mufflin Company, New York, 1916

Peare, Catherine Owens, *The Helen Keller Story*, Thomas Crowell Company, New York, 1959

Robinson, E. E., & Edwards, Paul C., *The Memoirs of Ray L. Wilbur*, Stanford University Press, Stanford, California, 1960

Starr, Kevin, *Inventing the Dream*, Oxford University Press, New York, 1985

Swanberg, W. A., *Pulitzer,* Charles Scribner's Sons, New York, 1967

Walker, Franklin, *A Literary History of Southern California*, University of California Press, Berkeley, 1950

Other References

Los Angeles Times . . . . *Riverside Daily Press*

New York Times . . . . *Riverside Enterprise*

Numerous periodicals, magazines, encyclopedias, and brochures.

Acknowledgments

I am indebted to a number of people for their valuable help and encouragement. My thanks to the staff of the Riverside Public Library, the Riverside Local History Resource Center supervised by Richard Hanks and assistants Bill Bell and Kevin Hallaran, and also Gladys Murphy, formerly with the University of California Riverside, Special Collections.

I appreciate the wonderful stories Jane Margison and Bill Powell shared about their years of employment at the Mission Inn. I am grateful to friends, strangers and organizations who helped in many ways and allowed me the use of their photographs. I wish to especially thank Alan Curl and Kevin Hallaran for their valuable assistance and expertise.

Index